·BUILD·IT·BETTER·YOURSELF·
WOODWORKING PROJECTS

Jigs, Fixtures, and Shop Furniture

Collected and Written
by Nick Engler

Rodale Press
Emmaus, Pennsylvania

Printed in the United States of America

Series Editor: William H. Hylton
Managing Editor/Author: Nick Engler
Graphic Designer: Linda Watts
Draftspersons: Mary Jane Favorite
                 Chris Walendzak
Photography: Karen Callahan
Cover Photography: Mitch Mandel
Proofreader: Hue Park
Typesetting by Computer Typography, Huber Heights, Ohio
Interior Illustrations by O'Neil & Associates, Dayton, Ohio
Endpaper Illustrations by Mary Jane Favorite
Produced by Bookworks, Inc., West Milton, Ohio

If you have any questions or comments concerning this book, please write:
Rodale Press
Book Reader Service
33 East Minor Street
Emmaus, PA 18098

Library of Congress Cataloging-in-Publication Data

Engler, Nick.
   Jigs, fixtures, and shop furniture/collected and written by Nick Engler; [photographer, Karen Callahan].
       p.   cm.—(Build-it-better-yourself woodworking projects)
  ISBN 0–87857–839–0 hardcover
  ISBN 0–87857–840–4 paperback
  1. Woodworking tools. 2. Woodwork—Equipment and supplies.
  I. Title. II. Series.
  TT186.E54 1989
  684'.08'028—dc20   89–6393
                               CIP

Distributed in the book trade by St. Martin's Press

    16 18 20 19 17   hardcover
4 6 8 10 9 7 5 3   paperback

Contents

Making Jigs, Fixtures, and Shop Furniture

As do all precision machines, your workshop tools each have a *design envelope*. A table saw, for example, has specific capacities and capabilities dictated by its engineering — the diameter of the blade, the size of the work surface, the horsepower of the motor, and so on. You can only do so much within that envelope. There are limits to the types of cuts you can make with your table saw, and to the sizes of the materials that it will handle.

The purpose of a jig or a fixture is to help you "push the edges of the envelope" — safely. These homemade accessories extend the capacity or augment the capability of a tool *without* endangering the operator or the machinery. Without jigs, most table saws can only make simple cuts in medium-sized workpieces. To cut smaller-than-normal boards, for instance, you must place your fingers too close to the blade for safety. Also, the blade may fling the cut pieces at you. However, you can use a *pushstick* to feed the work without risking your fingers and a *fingerboard* to prevent kickback. These simple jigs expand the saw's design envelope to encompass small workpieces. Other jigs and fixtures will help you handle large workpieces, and still others facilitate sawing operations you couldn't otherwise do.

A good piece of shop furniture also extends the envelope, though in a different way. Straight out of the box, few tools provide storage for materials and accessories. Adequate storage, however, is essential in a woodworking shop. With no way to organize your tools and keep them handy, your work proceeds slowly and uncertainly. A properly designed tool stand or cabinet adds the storage capacity you need to work efficiently.

There are plans for more than three dozen jigs, fixtures and furniture pieces in this book, divided into six areas of woodworking interest — safety, shop furniture, sawing, drilling, routing, and joinery. Each of these projects is designed to increase the capability and capacity of your workshop in an important way. Many have dozens of applications, and will push the edges of a tool's design envelope in several directions at once. As you come across operations in your woodworking that seem difficult to perform or beyond the ability of your tools, consult this book. Chances are, the jigs and fixtures here will help you do what you want to do.

Precision

As you build jigs or fixtures, remember that these are accessories to your tools. As such, they must be made as precisely as your tools — especially those that provide working or guiding surfaces, such as the *router table* or *tall fence extension*. To achieve the necessary precision you need, do several things:

■ Before you cut or drill wood, check the alignment and the adjustment of your tools. Make sure that blades, bits, tables, and fences are at the proper angles to one another.

■ Keep your pencil sharp. This may sound funny, but your pencil is probably the most inaccurate tool in your shop. As it dulls, the lines you mark get wider. The wider the line, the less accurate it is. A mark made by a dull pencil can throw off a cut as much as $1/16''$. Furthermore, if a line is long, it may widen noticeably as the pencil point wears down. To avoid these problems altogether, use an awl or metal scribe. Neither dulls quickly. The line either marks is always the same width. And there's an added bonus: When properly sharpened, an awl or scribe cuts the wood grain, which helps prevent chipping and tearing when you make the cut.

■ Always use the same measuring tool. If you have a favorite tape measure or straightedge, keep it handy and use it throughout a project. Even if you prefer to use a different measuring device for certain operations (such as a step-gauge to set the height of a saw blade), double-check your setup or your cut marks with your favorite measuring tool. The reason is not that the measurements on one tool differ from those on another. It's because the style of the markings differ, and you may not read one set of markings the same way you read another. Also, as a measuring tool becomes more familiar, it becomes easier to read.

■ No matter what kind of measuring tool you use, always read it straight on, not from an angle. If you constantly change the direction and the angle at which you read the markings, your measurements will be inaccurate. If you can, use a thin, flat tool such as a tape. These are more accurate than thick metal or wooden rules.

Materials

Once you build a precision jig or fixture, you want it to remain precise. Wooden projects, however, expand and contract with changes in temperature and humidity. This can cause a jig to warp or twist, making it useless. So choose your materials carefully. There are three common materials that are particularly well-suited for jigs and fixtures — close-grained hardwood, cabinet-grade hardwood plywood, and laminate-covered particleboard.

Close-grained hardwoods, such as birch or maple, don't absorb or release moisture as quickly as softwoods or woods with open grains. Consequently, they are more stable — they don't expand or contract as much as other woods. They're also easier to seal with a finish. This further slows moisture absorption and release, making the material that much more stable.

Birch and maple are also very hard woods. They stand up well to constant use (and abuse). Their density makes them particularly good for small jigs that you will use often, such as *fingerboards* and *miter gauge extensions.* If properly finished, jigs made from birch and maple remain serviceable for years. Softer close-grained hardwoods, such as poplar, may wear out quickly.

Cabinet-grade hardwood plywood is more stable than close-grained hardwood. Usually made from laminated layers (or plies) of poplar or luan mahogany, this plywood is faced with a hardwood veneer. Both poplar and mahogany are fairly stable woods, and the cross-grain layering of the plies enhances this. The trade-off is that plywood isn't very hard. The hardwood veneer provides some extra strength, but not enough to protect it from really hard knocks.

Still, it's well-suited for most jigs and fixtures, especially those in which you need large, flat guiding surfaces such as the *resawing fence* and the *miter jig.* You can also use it for most of the shop furniture projects in this book. If you build a shelf or a worktable from it, trim the edges with hard wood, as shown on the *table saw shelves.* This will help protect the most vulnerable areas of the project. It will also hide the plies and give your work a more finished look.

Note: Don't use construction-grade plywood, or plywood made from fir. Even though the wood is laminated in cross-grain layers, it's not as stable. It's also much softer than cabinet-grade plywood.

Laminate-covered particleboard, such as that used to make kitchen and bathroom countertops, is the most stable of the three materials mentioned. The laminate provides an exceptionally smooth, flat surface that is impervious to glue, finishes, and most other chemicals. Because of this, it's exceptionally good for making large worktables. As an added bonus, it's inexpensive. You can buy sink cut-outs at most building supply stores for just a few dollars. These are usually large enough to make good-sized worktables.

This material has its drawbacks, however. It's fairly fragile. Although the laminate itself is quite hard, the particleboard chips easily. If you make a worktable from it, you should protect the edges with hard wood, as was done on the *router table.* You must also be careful how you machine it. When you cut it to size, always make sure the laminate side faces *up* on your table saw or radial arm saw. Don't use a dado cutter; it will chip the laminate. Use a router instead.

In addition to choosing your materials carefully, you should also give some thought to how you assemble them. Glue most joints *and* reinforce them with screws — the screws act like miniature clamps, holding the pieces together even if the glue fails. If the wood is too thin or fragile for screws, use nails or brads. When making a jig that's to be used near a blade or a cutter, and there's a chance that you may saw through the jig — either accidentally or on purpose — use brass screws and hardware. Brass is a soft metal. If you happen to cut through a screw, it won't ruin the cutting edge of your tool.

Finishes

Your jigs and fixtures will last a lot longer if you apply a finish to them, especially those made from solid hardwood. A finish seals the wood against moisture, and helps minimize shrinking and swelling. It also prevents the wood from drying out too much and becoming brittle.

Use a finish that penetrates the wood, such as Danish oil or tung oil. Varnishes and other finishes that build up on the wood surface may interfere with the jig's action, or they may prevent a workpiece from sliding easily across its surface. Furthermore, they scratch easily and eventually wear off. To scratch a penetrating finish, you must cut the wood deeply. And the finish will last until the wood itself wears away.

Follow up the penetrating finish with several coats of paste wax. This further seals the wood and keeps glue from sticking to the surface. It also helps workpieces glide smoothly across worktables, fences, and guides. Whenever the wooden jig looks dull or workpieces won't slide easily, apply another coat of wax.

Designing Your Own Jigs and Fixtures

As you work with the projects in this book, you may wish to modify them so that they work better with your own tools. Or you may develop ideas for new jigs, fixtures, and shop furniture. When you design and build your own workshop accessories, here are two important tips to help ensure your success:

■ *Keep it simple.* You don't want to spend more time making the jig than you do working with it. You also want the jig to be precise. The more parts a jig has, the greater the chance that it won't be. Each part requires several cuts, and each cut is slightly inaccurate, no matter how carefully you align your tools. The inaccuracies add up as you add parts.

■ *Don't push the envelope too far.* While jigs and fixtures will greatly expand your capabilities, there are some things you just can't do safely. Use your common sense. Don't push a tool or yourself beyond safe limits.

Safety Tools

- Pushsticks
- Sawdust Collectors
- Worklight
- Saw Stand
- Fingerboards

While being a careful craftsman is your best protection in the workshop, you can get help from some homemade tools — pushsticks, sawdust collectors, a worklight, a saw stand, and fingerboards.

Each of these simple-to-make tools defends you against a different shop hazard. *Pushsticks* extend your reach without putting your hands and fingers near whirling blades and cutters. *Sawdust collectors* reduce the clutter, making your shop environment safer and more pleasant. A *worklight* helps you to see your work — and how close your hands are to the blades and cutters. A *saw stand* supports workpieces that would otherwise be too large to handle safely. *Fingerboards* hold the work down on the table or against a fence. And, in addition to the protection they offer, all of these tools help you work more easily and accurately.

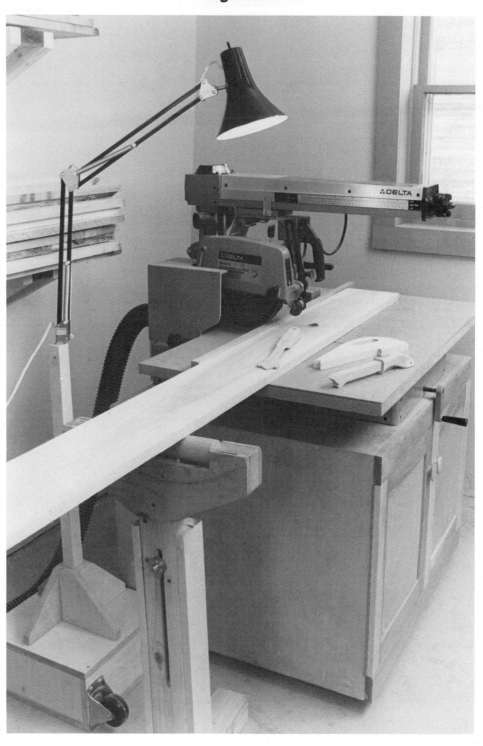

Pushsticks

Every power tool (or, for that matter, any tool with moving parts) has one or more danger zones — areas where you cannot put your fingers, hands, or other parts of your body without risk. Keep yourself outside these areas, away from the exposed cutting edge, and you'll be relatively safe. Once inside the danger zone, the slightest miscalculation can cause serious injury.

Pushsticks will reach inside a danger zone for you whenever you need to maneuver stock close to a blade, cutter, or bit. They increase your control and accuracy when cutting small and medium-sized parts. They're particularly useful when finishing a cut — pushing the end of a board past a blade or cutter. Each of the three pushsticks shown serves a slightly different purpose. The contoured pushstick is for general work — it fits the hand comfortably. The

reversible pushstick controls narrow or thin stock in between a rip fence and a blade or cutter. The pushstick/shoe serves double duty: In addition to pushing, it will also hold

a board flat on a worktable. Make several of each, and place them in easy-to-reach places around your shop, so there will always be a pushstick on hand when you need one.

Materials List

FINISHED DIMENSIONS

PARTS

A. Contoured
    pushstick   1½" x 1½" x 11½"
B. Reversible
    pushstick   ¾" x 2⅜" x 11¾"
C. Pushstick/shoe   ¾" x 4⅜" x 12¼"

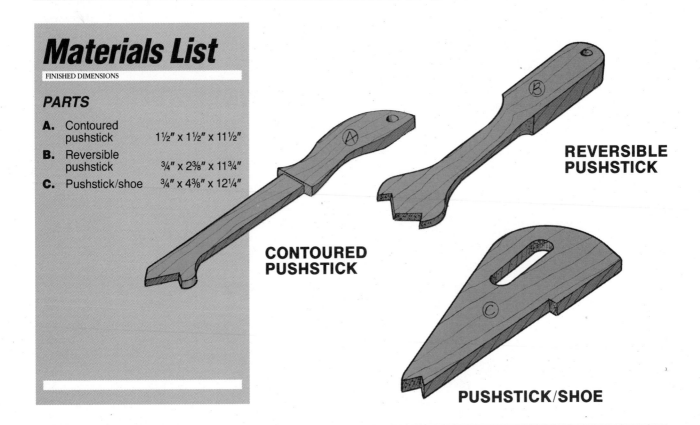

CONTOURED PUSHSTICK

REVERSIBLE PUSHSTICK

PUSHSTICK/SHOE

Making the Contoured Pushstick

1 **Select the stock.** These safety tools are small enough to be made from scrap wood, but don't use *scrappy* wood. A pushstick made from rough lumber with knots, checks, or other defects may come apart in your hands. Choose clear, straight-grained wood.

2 **Cut the shape.** Cut the stock slightly larger than shown in the Materials List. Enlarge the *Contoured Pushstick Patterns*. Trace the top pattern on the edge of the stock, and the side pattern on the face.

Make sure the shoulders of both patterns (where the handle meets the shaft) line up.

Drill a ¼″-diameter hole through the handle, as shown on the side pattern. (You can use this hole to hang up the pushstick.) Cut the side pattern on a band saw, but save the waste. Tape it back to the workpiece, making the block rectangular again, and cut the top pattern. (See Figure 1.) When you remove the tape and the waste, you'll have the rough shape of the pushstick.

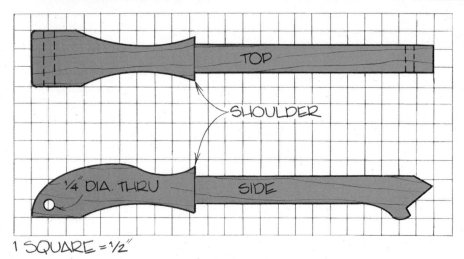

1/Form the contours of the pushstick with compound cuts on a band saw. After cutting the side pattern, tape the waste back to the stock and cut the top pattern.

TRY THIS! When making compound cuts on the band saw, use double-faced carpet tape to stick the waste to the workpiece. The tape holds the pieces together without obscuring your pattern lines, and it's thick enough to fill the kerf left by the band saw blade.

TOP

SHOULDER

¼″ DIA. THRU   SIDE

1 SQUARE = ½″

CONTOURED PUSHSTICK PATTERNS

3 **Smooth the contours.** With a rasp and sandpaper, smooth the handle. Remove the saw marks and round over the corners so the pushstick fits your hand comfortably.

Making the Reversible Pushstick

1 **Cut the shape.** Like the contoured pushstick, the reversible pushstick is formed with compound cuts on a band saw. Cut the stock slightly larger than shown in the Materials List. Enlarge the *Reversible Pushstick Patterns*. Trace the top pattern on the edge of the stock, and the side pattern on the face.

Make sure both patterns line up, with the handle portions facing in the same direction.

Drill a ¼″-diameter hole through the handle, as shown on the side pattern. This time, cut the top pattern first. Save the waste and tape it back to the workpiece. Cut the side pattern, then remove the tape and the waste.

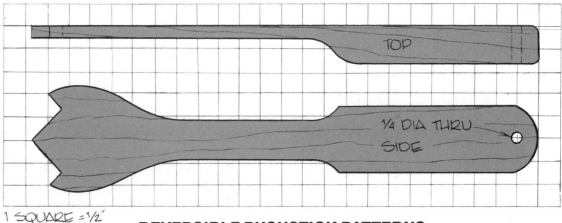

TOP

¼″ DIA THRU

SIDE

1 SQUARE = ½″

REVERSIBLE PUSHSTICK PATTERNS

2 **Smooth the contours.** With a rasp and sandpaper, smooth the handle. Remove the saw marks and round over the corners so the pushstick fits your hand comfortably.

Tips for Using the Reversible Pushstick

The reversible pushstick has a thin shaft to guide narrow workpieces between fence and blade. The tool is reversible (that is, you can flip it over). Always hold the pushstick with the handle protruding over the fence, *away* from the blade.

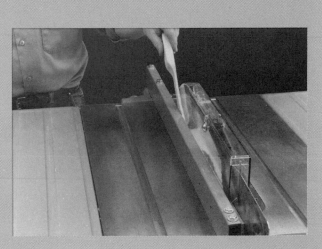

Making the Pushstick/Shoe

1 ***Cut the shape.*** Cut the stock slightly larger than shown in the Materials List. Enlarge the *Pushstick/Shoe Pattern* and trace it onto the face of the board. Cut the shape with a band saw or saber saw. Sand the edges to remove the saw marks.

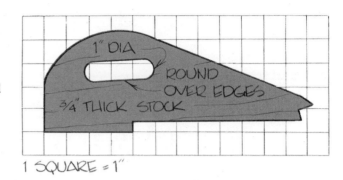

PUSHSTICK/SHOE PATTERN

2 ***Make the handle cutout.*** Drill two 1″-diameter holes, one at each end of the handle cutout. Remove the waste between the holes with a saber saw. Sand the edges to remove the saw marks, then round the corners of the handle so it fits your hand comfortably.

Sawdust Collectors

Sawdust poses several threats in a workshop. Piles of sawdust are accidents waiting to happen — you could lose your balance on one and fall into the machinery. They are fire hazards, too. Fine sawdust is a hazard to machinery. It can work its way into bushings and bearings (even sealed bearings!), drying them and causing excessive wear. Finally, sawdust is hazardous to your health. Fine dust particles irritate your eyes, nose, and lungs. Sawdust from several common types of stock, such as cedar and pressure-treated wood, is toxic. This is particularly dangerous if you suffer from asthma, emphysema, or allergies.

To reduce the danger, collect sawdust *as you work*. The devices shown will collect the dust from four common power tools — table saw, radial arm saw, jointer, and band saw — *before* it is thrown into the air or onto the floor. Simply hook the hose of your shop vacuum to a sawdust collector, then run the vacuum as you use the tool.

Materials List

FINISHED DIMENSIONS

PARTS

Table Saw/Jointer Dust Collector

A. Base   ¾″ x (variable) x (variable)
B. Front   ¾″ x 9″* x (variable)
C. Sides (2)   ¾″ x 9″* x (variable)
D. Back   ¾″ x (variable) x (variable)
E. Bottom   ¼″ x (variable) x (variable)

*6″ for jointer

Radial Arm Saw Dust Collector

A. Base   ¾″ x 5½″ x (variable)
B. Outer side   ¼″ x (variable) x (variable)
C. Inner side   ¼″ x (variable) x (variable)
D. Back   ¾″ x 5½″ x (variable)
E. Top   ¼″ x 5½″ x (variable)

Band Saw Dust Collector

A. Collet   3½″ dia. x ¾″

HARDWARE

Table Saw/Jointer Dust Collector

1½″ x (variable) Piano hinge and mounting screws
#10 x 1¼″ Flathead wood screws (8)
4d Finishing nails (10–12)
⅜″ Hooks and eyes (2)
⅜″ x 2″ Carriage bolts, lock washers, and nuts (4)

Radial Arm Saw Dust Collector

1″ Brads (15–20)
⅜″ x 2″ Carriage bolts, lock washers, and nuts (2)

Band Saw Dust Collector

#12 x 1¼″ Roundhead machine bolts, lock washers, and nuts (4)

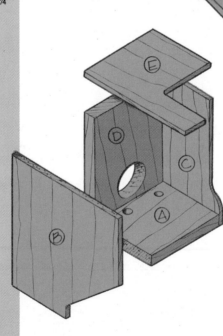

RADIAL ARM SAW DUST COLLECTOR EXPLODED VIEW

TABLE SAW/JOINTER DUST COLLECTOR EXPLODED VIEW

BAND SAW DUST COLLECTOR ISOMETRIC VIEW

Making the Table Saw and Jointer Dust Collectors

1 **Determine the dimensions.** This design will work on most table saws and jointers, but the dimensions will vary depending on the brand and the model of your tool. They will also vary depending on the tool stand, the size and location of the motor, the pulleys and V-belts, and other hardware. Unplug the tool and vacuum up any sawdust. Inspect the underside of the tool and determine how you will attach the dust collector. Note the position of the motor and look for unusual protrusions — you may have to fit the dust collector around them.

Carefully measure the opening at the base of the tool, where you will attach the collector. If necessary, cut a cardboard template for the dust collector base, and fit it to the underside of the tool. When you are sure of your measurements, determine the dimensions of the dust collector parts.

2 **Cut the parts.** Rip and cut the parts — base, side, front, back, and bottom — to the sizes you need. Taper the sides and bevel the bottom edges of the front and back at 20°. Also, bevel the front and back edges of the bottom.

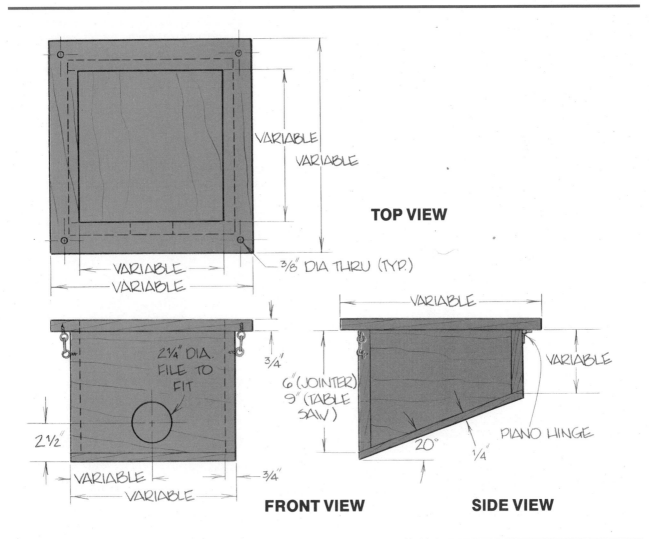

TOP VIEW

VARIABLE
VARIABLE

VARIABLE
VARIABLE

3/8" DIA THRU (TYP.)

2¼" DIA. FILE TO FIT

¾"

2½"

VARIABLE
VARIABLE

¾"

6" (JOINTER)
9" (TABLE SAW)

20°

¼"

VARIABLE

PIANO HINGE

VARIABLE

FRONT VIEW

SIDE VIEW

3 **Make the base.** Drill ⅜″-diameter holes in the base where you will bolt it to the table saw or jointer. Mark the area that you want to cut out. Drill a ¼″-diameter hole at each corner of this area, then cut from hole to hole with a saber saw to remove the waste. (See Figure 1.)

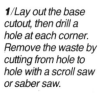

1/Lay out the base cutout, then drill a hole at each corner. Remove the waste by cutting from hole to hole with a scroll saw or saber saw.

4 **Cut the vacuum hole.** Using a hole saw, cut a 2¼″-diameter hole in the front as shown in the *Front View.* Test fit the end of a standard 2½″ vacuum hose in the hole. It should fit snugly. If the hole is too small, rasp or file the edge until the hose fits properly. If it's too large, glue shims to the edge of the hole.

5 **Assemble the dust collector.** Glue the sides, front, and back together. Reinforce the joints with screws. Glue the bottom to the assembly, then tack it in place with finishing nails. Let the glue dry, then sand all the joints flush and clean.

Clamp the assembled dust bin to the base, and install a piano hinge at the back. Attach hooks and eyes to the front corners to keep the bin up against the base. The hooks must hold the bin *tightly,* so no dust can leak out.

6 **Attach the dust collector to the tool.** If necessary, drill holes in the tool or the tool stand for the bolts. (You may have to remove the tool or the motor — or both — from the tool stand to do this.) Bolt the dust collector in place, using lock washers on the bolts to be sure the collector doesn't vibrate loose.

Tips for Using the Table Saw/Jointer Dust Collector

With this collector attached, you *must* run the vacuum whenever you run the tool. If you don't, the bin may become clogged with dust and chips. If it does become clogged, pull the hooks from the eyes, allowing the bin to swing down. Remove the debris, then hook the bin back against the base.

Making the Radial Arm Saw Dust Collector

1 **Determine the dimensions.** Like the table saw/jointer dust collector, the radial arm saw dust collector must be customized to fit your particular saw. Study the plans shown, then inspect your tool. Decide how you will attach the collector to the table frame. Once you have decided this, you can determine how deep to make the base of the collector.

Calculate the height of the collector. When installed, the top should be 1″–2″ above the saw arbor. If you make the height of the sides approximately 4/5 (80%) of the diameter of the saw blade, this should put the top

where you want it. If you have a 10″ saw, make the sides 8″ tall. Measure the tool to see if this will work for you. If not, adjust the height up or down.

Finally, determine the depth of the sides. The outer side should extend 1″–2″ forward of the back edge of the saw guard, when the saw is pushed all the way back. The inner side should be ½″ short of the guard.

Once you settle on the overall dimensions of the collector, calculate the measurements and plan the shape of each part. Sketch a full-size plan for the top and the sides.

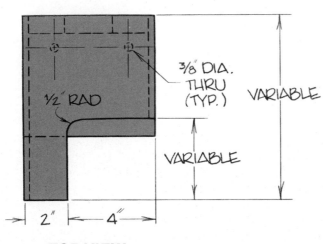

TOP VIEW

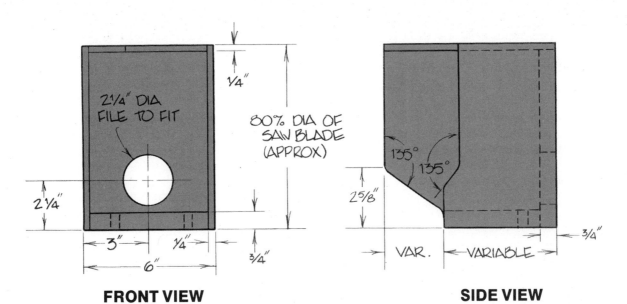

FRONT VIEW   **SIDE VIEW**

2

Cut the parts. Cut the top, base, sides, and back to size. This collector is assembled with butt joints, so all the edges will be square.

Using the plans you've drawn, mark the shapes of the top and the sides on the stock. Cut the shapes with a band saw or saber saw, and smooth the sawed edges. Drill ⅜″-diameter holes in the base so you can bolt it to the saw frame. **Note:** On some saws, you may find it easier to attach the collector with metal brackets.

3

Cut the vacuum hole. Using a hole saw, cut a 2¼″-diameter hole in the back as shown in the *Front View.* Test fit the end of a standard 2½″ vacuum hose in the hole. It should fit snugly. If the hole is too small, rasp or file the edge until the hose fits properly. If it's too large, glue shims to the edge of the hole.

4

Assemble the collector and attach it to the saw. Glue the parts together, reinforcing the joints with brads. Let the glue dry, then sand all joints clean and flush.

Set up the radial arm saw to make a 90° crosscut. (Both the blade angle and the arm angle should be set to 0°.) Place the collector on the saw frame, directly behind the saw. The top's edge should be about ½″ from the saw guard.

Temporarily clamp the collector to the frame. Set up the saw to cut a miter. (Change the arm angle to 45°, but leave the blade angle a 0°.) Check that the collector doesn't touch the saw guard or interfere with the movement of the saw. (See Figure 1.) If it does, move it slightly or trim away the inner side and the top with a saber saw.

When you're sure the collector will not interfere with the saw, remove it. Drill bolt holes in the frame, then attach the collector permanently to the radial arm saw.

1/With the dust collector clamped to the frame, check the action of the radial arm saw. If the collector interferes with the saw, move it or trim the top and inner side.

Use lock washers on the bolts to keep the collector from vibrating loose.

Making the Band Saw Dust Collector

1

Make the collet. On your band saw, cut a ¾″-thick disk, 3½″ in diameter from hardwood or plywood. Using a hole saw, cut a 2¼″-diameter hole, centered in the stock. Test fit the end of a standard 2½″ vacuum hose to the hole. It should fit snugly. If the hole is too small, rasp or file the edge until the hose fits properly. If it's too large, glue shims to the edge of the hole. When the vacuum hole is properly sized, drill four ³/₁₆″-diameter holes, evenly spaced around the collet as shown in the *Front View.*

2 *Attach the collet to the band saw.*

Remove the lower wheel cover from your band saw. (Some band saws have just one cover for both wheels.) Cut a 2¼"-diameter hole in the cover, near the bottom edge and toward the front of the saw. (The exact position is not critical.) To make this hole, use either a fly cutter mounted on your drill press or a saber saw with a metal-cutting blade. Put the collet in place over the hole and mark the position of the ³/₁₆"-diameter bolt holes. Drill these holes.

Bolt the collet to the wheel cover, and reinstall the cover on the saw. Spin the wheels by hand to make sure the collet bolts don't rub the wheel rim or hit the spokes. If they do, file down the ends or replace them with shorter bolts.

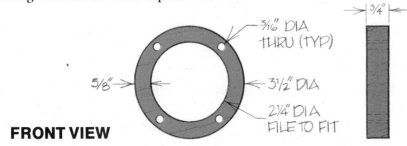

³/₁₆" DIA
THRU (TYP)

5/8"

3½" DIA

2¼" DIA
FILE TO FIT

¾"

FRONT VIEW   **SIDE VIEW**

Worklight

Because most home workshops are located in basements or garages, the lighting is often very poor. When you consider the dangers, you understand how foolish it is to work in poor light. Workshops should be lit as well as operating rooms. You must be able to see where your hands are in relation to blades, cutters, and bits at *all times*.

This roll-around worklight reduces the hazard. It is a tension lamp (sometimes called a multipurpose lamp) mounted on a mobile base. Move the stand next to the tool or bench where you need extra light, then position the lamp over the work.

Materials List

FINISHED DIMENSIONS

PARTS

A. Top/base (2)   ¾" x 14" x 14"
B. Sides (4)   ¾" x 5" x 13¼"
C. Braces (4)   ¾" x 6" x 7¼"
D. Post   1½" x 1½" x 29½"

HARDWARE

Tension Lamp

#10 x 1¼" Flathead wood screws
   (24–30)
4" Fixed casters and mounting
   screws (2)

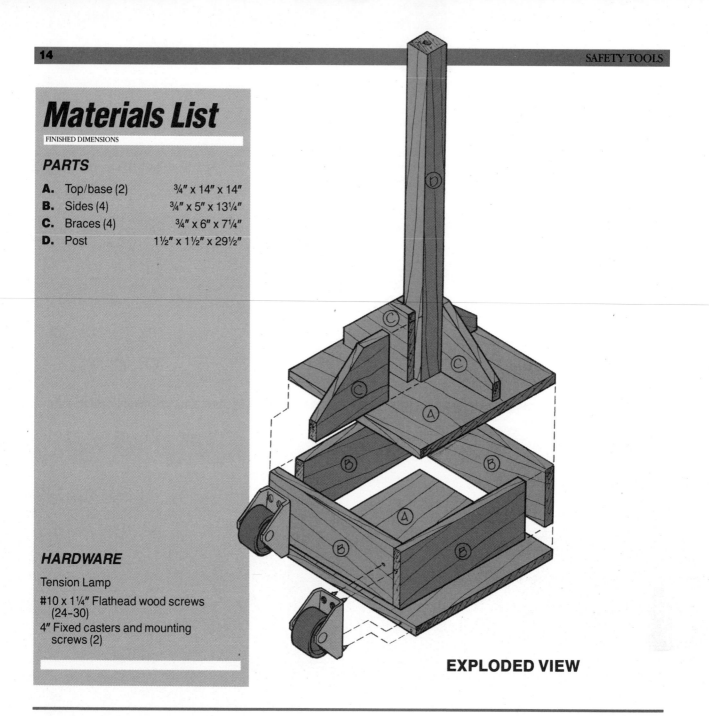

EXPLODED VIEW

1 **Cut the parts.** Glue up wide stock for the top
and base (or use scraps of plywood, if you wish),
then cut the parts to the sizes in the Materials List. Cut
a corner off each brace, as shown in the *Brace Layout*.

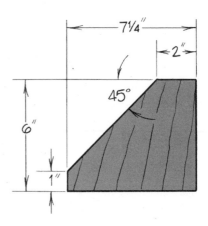

7¼"

2"

45°

6"

1"

BRACE LAYOUT

2

Assemble the base. Glue the sides together, and reinforce the joints with screws. Screw (but don't glue) the base to the side assembly. Sand all joints clean and flush.

3

Assemble the top. Measure the mounting shaft at the base of your tension lamp. (Most have ½″-diameter shafts.) Drill a hole in the top end of the post, the same length and diameter as the shaft.

Glue the braces to the bottom of the post and reinforce the joints with screws. Screw (but don't glue) the post assembly to the top. (This will allow you to remove the top and add weight inside the base assembly.)

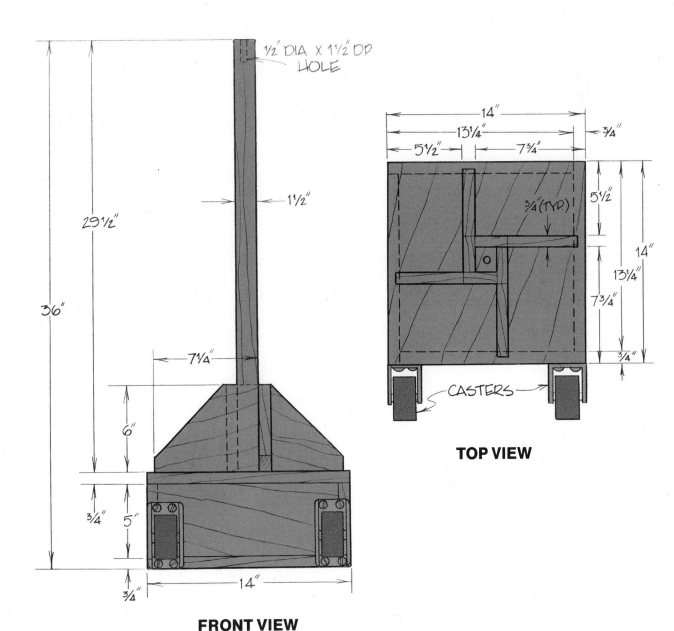

FRONT VIEW

TOP VIEW

4 Assemble the worklight.

Assemble the worklight. Attach *fixed* casters to one side of the box. The edge of these casters must be flush with the bottom of the base, as shown in the *Front View.* This will make the worklight easy to move around your shop. (See Figure 1.)

To make the light as stable as possible, remove the post assembly and place several bricks or a few shovels of gravel in the base. Screw the top portion to the base and mount the tension lamp in the top of the post.

1/To move the worklight around the shop, tilt it back on its casters. These casters must be **fixed** — swivel casters will not work.

Saw Stand

Ripping an 8'-long (or longer) board on the typical home-shop table saw is difficult, even hazardous. You need someone to support the board as it comes off the saw. Someone or something…like this saw stand.

A saw stand is a roller mounted on a movable platform. The roller can be adjusted so it is level with the working surface of a power tool or workbench. The stand shown uses a wooden rolling pin for a roller. The base has three feet, so the saw stand will rest solidly on any surface.

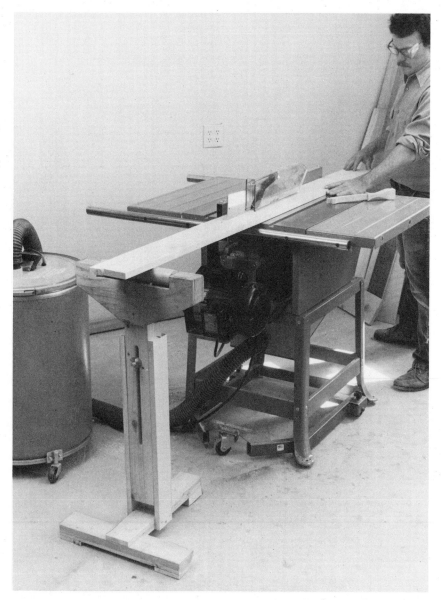

EXPLODED VIEW

Materials List

FINISHED DIMENSIONS

PARTS

A. Base/crossbar (2)   1½" x 3½" x 18"

B. Large foot   1¼" x 3½" x 3½"

C. Small feet (2)   ½" x 3½" x 3½"

D. Stationary post   1½" x 3½" x 20½"

E. Sliding post   1½" x 3⅜" x 25½"

F. Guides (2)   ¾" x 3" x 22"

G. Roller supports (2) ½" x 6½" x 17"

H. Roller mounting
   blocks (2)   1½" x 3¼" x 3½"

HARDWARE

10"-long Hardwood rolling pin
#10 x 1¼" Flathead wood screws
   (24–30)
½" x 4½" Carriage bolt, fender washer,
   and wing nut

---

1 ***Cut the parts.*** To make this project, you need approximately 3 board feet of ¾" utility lumber, a few scraps of ½" plywood, and a 2 x 4 x 8'. The grade and the appearance of the ¾ lumber and the plywood is not critical, but the 2 x 4 *must* be clear and straight.

Clear 2 x 4's are available at most lumberyards, though they cost a good deal more than construction-grade 2 x 4's. When you have gathered the stock, cut all the parts to the sizes shown on the Materials List.

2 Make the roller supports and mounting blocks.

Depending on the rolling pin, you may need to change the shape of the roller support sightly. Measure the length and radius of the rolling pin. The notch for it at the top of the support should be ¼″ longer than it is (excluding the handles) and ⅞″ deeper than its radius. Make any changes necessary to the *Roller Support Layout* and trace the layout on ½″ plywood. Cut out the shape of the supports with a band saw or saber saw.

Pry the wooden handles off the rolling pin. These are pressed onto a metal axle that runs through the rolling pin, and they will come off with a little force. (See Figure 1.) Measure the diameter of the axle and the length that extends from either end of the pin. Drill stopped holes to fit the axle in the inside edges of the roller mounting blocks, as shown in the *Roller Mounting Block Details*. Chamfer the lower outside corner of each block so it fits neatly between the roller supports.

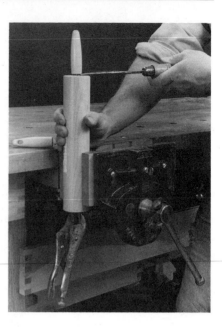

1/Use a small screwdriver to remove the handles from the rolling pin. When removing the second handle, clamp locking-grip pliers to the exposed axle (where you just removed the first handle). This will keep the axle from pulling out of the pin.

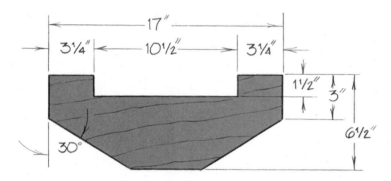

**ROLLER SUPPORT
LAYOUT**

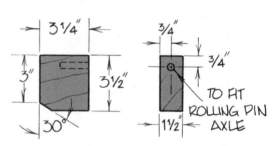

**ROLLER MOUNTING BLOCK
DETAILS**

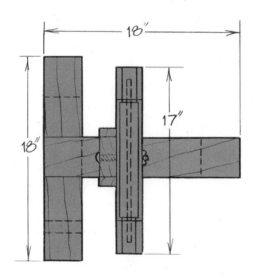

TOP VIEW

3

Cut the slot in the sliding post. Lay out a 9/16"-wide, 12"-long slot on the sliding post as shown in the *Sliding Post Layout*. Drill two 9/16"-diameter holes to mark the ends of this slot, then remove the waste between the holes with a saber saw. (See Figure 2.) File the inside edges of the slot smooth.

9/16" WD SLOT THRU

1 11/16"

TOP

3 3/8"

5 1/2" 12" 7"

25 1/2"

SLIDING POST LAYOUT

2/Cut the slot in the sliding post with a saber saw and a long, stiff blade. Take it slow; a saber saw blade tends to lean one way or the other in thick stock if you feed it too fast, especially when you're cutting with the grain. If this happens, the inside edges of the slot will be beveled and the width will be uneven.

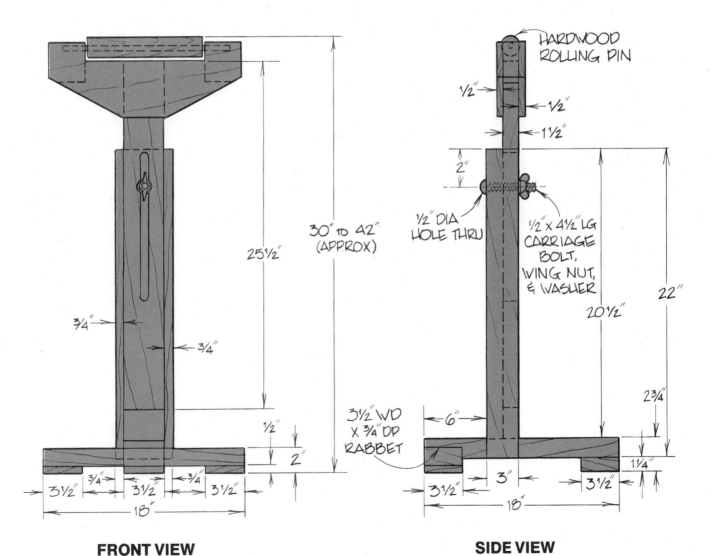

HARDWOOD ROLLING PIN

1/2" 1/2" 1 1/2" 2"

1/2" DIA HOLE THRU

1/2" x 4 1/2" LG CARRIAGE BOLT, WING NUT, & WASHER

30" to 42" (APPROX)

25 1/2"

3/4" 3/4"

1/2" 2"

3 1/2" 3/4" 3 1/2" 3/4" 3 1/2"

18"

20 1/2"

22"

2 3/4"

1 1/4"

3 1/2" WD X 3/4" DP RABBET

6"

3 1/2" 3" 3 1/2"

18"

FRONT VIEW

SIDE VIEW

4 **Cut a lap in the base.** Cut a 3½"-wide,
¾"-deep lap in one end of the base, where it
attaches to the crossbar. To do this, adjust the height of
your table saw or radial arm saw blade to cut ¾"-deep
kerfs in 1½"-thick stock. Make repeated cuts to form the
lap. (See Figure 3.)

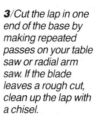

*3/Cut the lap in one
end of the base by
making repeated
passes on your table
saw or radial arm
saw. If the blade
leaves a rough cut,
clean up the lap with
a chisel.*

5 **Assemble the saw stand.** Glue the feet to
the bottom of the base and the crossbar. Let the
glue dry, then attach the base to the crossbar with glue
and screws.

Glue the guides to the stationary post so the tops of
the guides are flush with the top of the post. Reinforce
the joints with screws. Place the sliding post in between
the guides so the bottom of both posts are flush. With a
pencil, mark the *top* end of the slot on the inside face of
the stationary post. Remove the sliding post and drill a
½"-diameter hole at this mark for a carriage bolt. Glue
and screw the bottom portion of the guides to the base.

Insert the ends of the roller axle into the holes in the
mounting blocks. Glue the blocks and the top end of the
sliding post between the roller supports. Reinforce the
joints with screws.

Sand all joints clean and flush. Insert a carriage bolt
into the hole in the stationary post, as shown in the *Side
View.* Put the sliding post assembly in place, fitting the
slot over the bolt. Secure the sliding post with a fender
washer and wing nut.

Tips for Using the Saw Stand

To adjust the roller's height so it is level with a work
surface, place a long, straight board with one end on
the roller and the other on the surface. Raise or lower
the roller until the board rests flat on the work surface.
Tighten the wing nut to secure the roller.

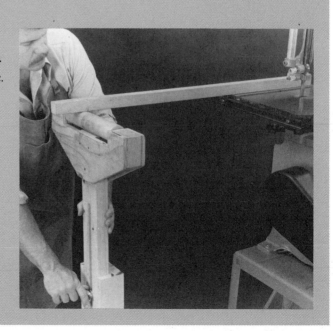

Fingerboards

A fingerboard (sometimes called a featherboard) serves two purposes: First, it helps to hold a workpiece against a table or fence as you feed the board into a blade or cutter. Second, it prevents the board from kicking back. This, in turn, makes your woodworking safer and more accurate.

There are two ways to use a fingerboard. If you need both your hands free to feed the work or operate the tool, clamp the fingerboards to the work surface or fence. If you have a free hand and cannot easily clamp the fingerboard to the tool, hold it in your hand, pressing it against the wood. Shown are two types of fingerboards, one designed to be clamped to a tool and the other to be hand-held.

CLAMP-ON FINGERBOARD

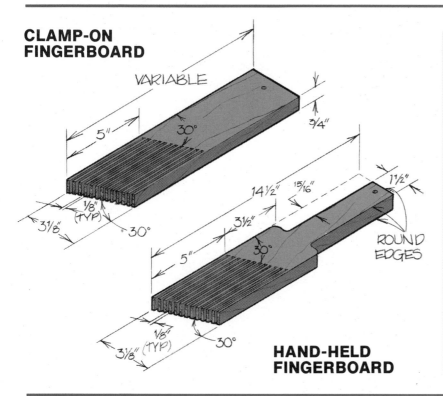

VARIABLE

5″

30°

3/4″

1/8″ (TYP)

3 1/8″

30°

14 1/2″   15/16″

3 1/2″

1 1/2″

5″

30°

ROUND EDGES

1/8″ (TYP)

3 1/8″

30°

HAND-HELD FINGERBOARD

Materials List

FINISHED DIMENSIONS

PARTS

A. Clamp-on fingerboard — (variable) x 3 1/8″ x (variable)

B. Hand-held fingerboard — 3/4″ x 3 1/8″ x 14 1/2″

1 Determine the size of the clamp-on fingerboard.

The optimum thickness and length of a clamp-on fingerboard changes from job to job and tool to tool. Generally, the larger your workpieces, the thicker the fingerboard should be. A 3/4″-thick fingerboard will supply adequate pressure for most small-to-medium work — picture frames, cabinet rails and stiles, and so on. But operations on larger pieces, such as resawing wide boards, will require more pressure — and a thicker fingerboard.

Where and how you clamp the fingerboard to the tool determines its length. Usually, you clamp the fingerboard near the edge of the worktable, with the fingers reaching in almost to the middle. A tool with a small worktable, such as a band saw or a drill press, requires a short fingerboard. A tool with a larger table, such as a table saw, needs something longer.

Determine the size that you need and cut the stock, mitering one end at 30°. Don't cut the fingerboard shorter than 7″. The fingers must be about 5″ long so they have the proper spring, and you need some stock at the base of the fingers to hold them together.

TRY THIS!   Make several different sizes of fingerboards — different lengths and different thicknesses — so you can choose the right one for each operation.

2 **Cut the fingers.**   Draw a line across the width of the fingerboard, parallel to the mitered end and 5″ from it. This marks the base of the fingers. Mount a combination blade — or any blade that cuts a ⅛″-wide kerf — in your table saw and position the rip fence ⅛″ away from it.

Turn the saw on and feed the mitered end of the fingerboard stock into the blade. Stop when the blade reaches the base line. Turn the saw off, move the rip fence ¼″ to the right (so it's ⅜″ away from blade) and cut another kerf, again stopping at the base line. (See Figure 1.) Repeat, moving the fence ¼″ at a time, until you reach the opposite edge of the stock and the fence

1/Make repetitive rip cuts to form the fingers. Each finger should be approximately ⅛″ wide.

is 2⅞″ away from the blade. These repetitive cuts will form ⅛″-wide fingers separated by ⅛″-wide kerfs in the mitered end of the stock.

3 **Cut the shape of the hand-held fingerboard.**   If you are making a hand-held fingerboard, cut the shape of the handle on a band saw or scroll saw. Round the corners of the handle with a file and sandpaper so it fits your hand comfortably.

Tips for Using Fingerboards

When using fingerboards, be careful where you place them — and make sure they stay in place.

If a clamp-on fingerboard shifts or creeps as you work, glue a piece of emery cloth to the underside of the board, just beneath the clamp. This cloth will grip the work surface (without scratching it) and keep the fingerboard stationary.

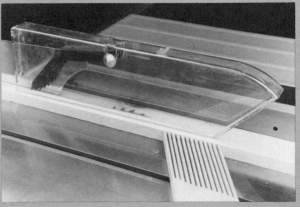

*Always position the fingerboards in **front** of the blade (on the infeed side) when ripping or cutting wood. If the fingers press the wood against the blade as it cuts, or squeeze the kerf closed in back of the blade, the blade will bind.*

Shop Furniture

- **Storage Stands**
- **Table Saw Shelves**
- **Tool Cabinet**
- **Wood Rack**

Your workshop presents enormous storage problems. How do you organize a dozen or so hand-held and stationary power tools, scores of hand tools, and hundreds of bits, cutters, accessories, fasteners, and materials? How do you keep them within easy reach of your work? How do you find one thing when you need it? Because you are continually wrestling with these problems, most shop furniture pieces are storage units.

The furniture in this chapter solves some of the most common storage problems. The *storage stands* convert wasted space — the space under your power tools — into storage space. There are plans for a drill press stand and a radial arm saw stand, but you can easily adapt these designs for many other tools. *Table saw shelves* hold your miter gauge and rip fence when they're not in use. The *tool cabinet* creates a place for the tools and materials you use most often. It can be moved easily around your shop, so you can keep your tools close at hand. The *wood rack* stores lots of wood in a small area, holding the boards horizontally. This prevents them from warping, and it gets them off the floor.

You can build all of these projects quickly from inexpensive materials, even the large cabinets and stands. This addresses two more storage problems — money and time. You can create a workshop storage system without spending a fortune or working a lifetime. ●

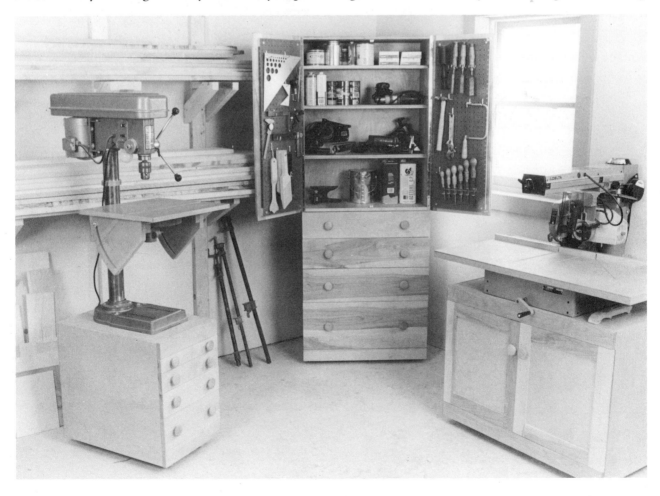

Storage Stands

If you're looking for extra space in your shop, there may be plenty under your stationary power tools. With a little wood and a little work, you can put the space to better use. Storage stands will support the tools *and* provide space to keep accessories and portable tools.

The cabinets shown support a radial arm saw and a drill press. However, these same designs will support other power tools. The drill press stand also supports a jointer at the proper height; the radial arm saw stand will hold a table saw or a lathe. Once you grasp the construction techniques, you can custom design your own stands for any stationary or benchtop power tool.

Both cabinets are equipped with casters, which permit you to move the units easily, an especially practical feature if your shop space is limited. Brakes on the casters prevent the tool from rolling away.

TRY THIS! For some tools, such as the jointer and the table saw, you may have to cut a hole in the cabinet top and place a large drawer below it to collect sawdust and chips.

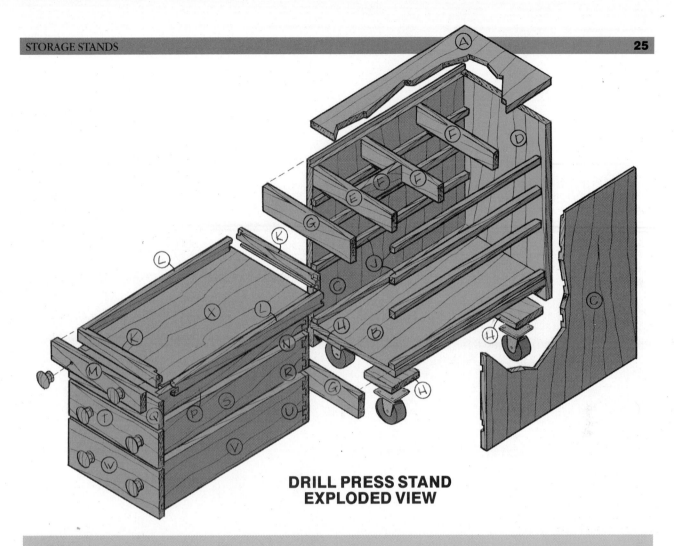

**DRILL PRESS STAND
EXPLODED VIEW**

Materials List

FINISHED DIMENSIONS

PARTS

A.	Top	¾" x 15¼" x 23¼"
B.	Bottom	¾" x 15¼" x 22½"
C.	Sides (2)	¾" x 22" x 23¼"
D.	Back	¾" x 15¼" x 21¼"
E.	Braces (3)	¾" x 2" x 14½"
F.	Kicker	¾" x 2" x 6¾"
G.	Front trim (2)	¾" x 2¾" x 16"
H.	Caster blocks (4)	¾" x 4" x 4"
J.	Drawer supports (8)	¾" x ¾" x 22½"
K.	Top drawer front/back (2)	¾" x 1⅝" x 14⅜"
L.	Top drawer sides (2)	¾" x 1⅝" x 21¾"
M.	Top drawer face	¾" x 2⅜" x 16"
N.	Upper middle drawer front/back (2)	¾" x 2⅝" x 14⅜"
P.	Upper middle drawer sides (2)	¾" x 2⅝" x 21¾"
Q.	Upper middle drawer face	¾" x 3⅜" x 16"
R.	Lower middle drawer front/back (2)	¾" x 3⅝" x 14⅜"
S.	Lower middle drawer sides (2)	¾" x 3⅝" x 21¾"
T.	Lower middle drawer face	¾" x 4⅜" x 16"
U.	Bottom drawer front/back (2)	¾" x 5⅛" x 14⅜"
V.	Bottom drawer sides (2)	¾" x 5⅛" x 21¾"
W.	Bottom drawer face	¾" x 5¾" x 16"
X.	Drawer bottoms (4)	¼" x 13⅝" x 21¾"

HARDWARE

2" Drawer pulls (8)
4" Casters with brakes and mounting screws (4)
#10 x 1¼" Flathead wood screws (36–48)
Hex-head bolts, to secure the tool base to the stand (3–4)

Making the Drill Press Stand

1 *Determine the dimensions.* The stand supports a bench drill press at a comfortable height for woodworking. Measure the base of your drill press to be sure it will fit on the stand. Also measure the height of the tool, and figure where the controls and the table will be. Will the stand, as shown, hold your drill press too low or too high? If so, make the proper changes in the plans and the Materials List.

2 *Cut the parts.* Purchase 4/4 birch lumber (for the trim and drawer faces) and cabinet-grade birch veneer plywood (for everything else) to make the cabinet. Plane the solid stock ¾″ thick. Then cut the parts for the case ("A" through "J" on the Materials List). Don't cut the drawer parts yet — there will be too many parts to keep track of.

TRY THIS! To keep plywood from tearing or splintering when you cut it, apply masking tape along the line you're about to cut. Redraw the line on top of the tape, and cut the wood. The tape will reinforce the veneer and keep the saw teeth from lifting the wood grain.

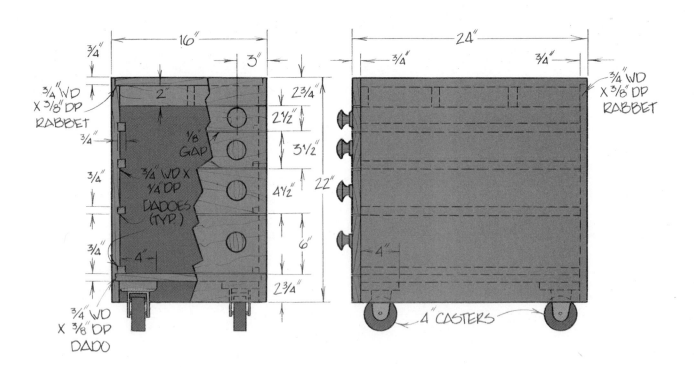

FRONT VIEW   **SIDE VIEW**

3

Cut the rabbets and dadoes. Assemble the case with rabbets and dadoes. Here's a list of the cuts you must make:

- ¾"-wide, ⅜"-deep rabbets in the back edges of the top and sides to hold the back
- ¾"-wide, ⅜"-deep rabbets in the top edges of the sides to hold the top
- ¾"-wide, ⅜"-deep dadoes in the sides to hold the bottom
- ¾"-wide, ¼"-deep dadoes in the sides to hold the drawer supports

Make all the joints with a router, a straight bit, and the T-square routing jig shown in the Routing chapter. Don't use a dado cutter; it will tear the veneer.

4

Assemble the case. To start, dry assemble the top, bottom, sides, and back to be sure they fit. When you're satisfied they do, join the top, bottom, and sides with glue and flathead wood screws. Counterbore and countersink each screw, then cover the head with a wooden plug. *Don't* glue the top in place yet. Just attach it with screws. Secure the back to the assembly, and let the glue set.

Remove the top. Glue the braces to the sides, then drive counterbored, countersunk screws through the sides into them. Attach the kicker between the front and middle braces (as shown in the *Top View*). Replace the top, gluing *and* screwing it to the case. Finally, attach the front trim pieces. When the glue dries, sand the joints and screw plugs clean and flush. Be careful not to sand too deep; you might sand through the plywood's veneer.

5

Install the drawer supports. Glue the drawer supports inside the case, each in a ¾"-wide, ¼"-deep dado. Wedge them in place while the glue dries. To do this, cut pieces of scrap slightly longer than the distance between a set of supports — about 13⅝". Place one end of the scrap against one support, then force the other end against the opposite support. After the glue dries, remove the scraps.

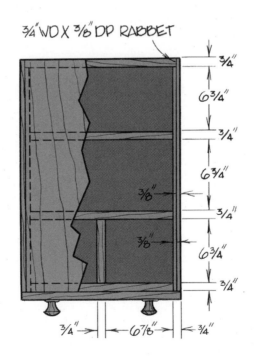

TOP VIEW

6

Install the casters. Glue and screw the caster blocks to the bottom of the case. Place the casters on the blocks and check that each caster swivels freely, without hitting any part of the case. Drill pilot holes for the mounting screws, and secure the casters to the caster blocks.

7

Make the drawers. Measure the inside of the case. Large projects have a way of changing dimension as you build them; you may have to adjust the sizes of the drawers somewhat. When you are sure of your dimensions, cut the drawer parts.

As the *Drawer/Side View* shows, each drawer front and back is joined to the sides with half-blind dovetails, and the bottom floats in grooves. Cut the grooves with a table-mounted router or a dado cutter, and the dovetails with a router and a dovetail jig. If you don't have this jig, use lock joints or rabbet joints instead of dovetails.

Assemble the front, back, and sides of each drawer with glue. Put the bottom in place when you put the drawer together, but don't glue it in the grooves. Let the glue dry, then sand the joints clean and flush.

SIDE VIEW

DRAWER

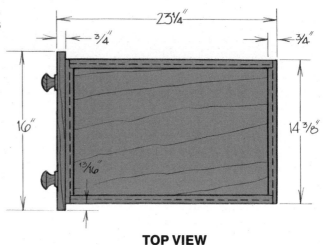

TOP VIEW

8

Attach the drawer faces and pulls. Place the drawers in the case and check that they slide in and out easily. If they bind, plane or sand the part that rubs.

Arrange the drawer faces over the drawers, using bar clamps to hold them against the edges of the case. Adjust their positions so the spacing between them is even. There should be a ⅛″ gap between adjacent faces, and the ends of each face should be flush with the case sides.

When the faces are properly positioned, mark the locations of the drawer pulls. Drill the holes for the mounting screws through the drawer faces *and* the drawer fronts.

Remove the clamps and the faces. Spread glue on the drawer fronts, then attach the faces and the drawer pulls. Pass the mounting bolt for each pull through *both* the front and the face, so the bolt holds the two parts together. Then clamp the faces to the drawers with hand screws. **Note:** The bolts that come with the pulls may not be long enough. If so, purchase 2″-long bolts to fit the pulls.

9

Apply a finish and attach the drill press. Lightly sand the completed stand, then apply an oil finish. When the finish dries, apply paste wax. The oil and wax prevent glue from sticking to the wood, and keep the stand from getting stained and dirty.

Place the drill press on top of the stand and position it so the base mounting holes are *not* directly over the braces. Mark these holes on the stand, then drill through the top. Bolt the tool to the stand, using lock washers to keep the bolts and nuts from vibrating loose.

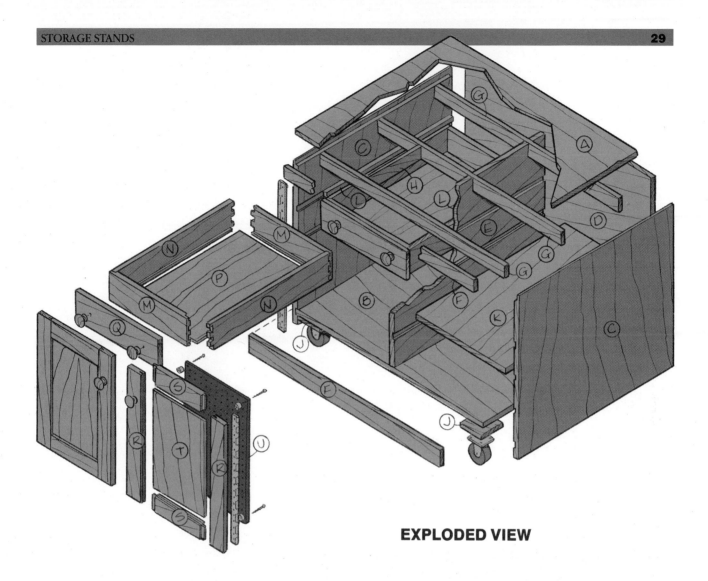

EXPLODED VIEW

Materials List

FINISHED DIMENSIONS

PARTS

A.	Top	¾″ x 29¼″ x 35¼″
B.	Bottom	¾″ x 28½″ x 34½″
C.	Sides (2)	¾″ x 26″ x 29¼″
D.	Back	¾″ x 25⅝″ x 35¼″
E.	Divider	¾″ x 23¼″ x 28½″
F.	Front trim (2)	¾″ x 2¾″ x 36″
G.	Braces (3)	¾″ x 2″ x 34½″
H.	Kicker	¾″ x 2″ x 10⅛″
J.	Caster blocks (4)	¾″ x 4″ x 4″
K.	Adjustable shelf	¾″ x 17½″ x 24½″
L.	Drawer supports (4)	¾″ x ¾″ x 23¾″
M.	Drawer fronts/ backs (4)	¾″ x 3⅞″ x 16¾″
N.	Drawer sides (4)	¾″ x 3⅞″ x 23″
P.	Drawer bottoms (2)	¼″ x 16″ x 23″
Q.	Drawer faces (2)	¾″ x 4⅝″ x 16¾″
R.	Door stiles (4)	¾″ x 2½″ x 20⅜″
S.	Door rails (4)	¾″ x 2½″ x 13¹⁵⁄₁₆″
T.	Door panels (2)	¼″ x 16¼″ x 13¹³⁄₁₆″
U.	Pegboard panels (2)	¼″ x 16″ x 18½″

HARDWARE

2″ Door/drawer pulls (6)

1½″ x 20⅜″ Piano hinges and mounting screws (1 pair)

Cabinet door catches (2)

¼″ I.D. Pipe (5″–6″)

#12 x 1½″ Roundhead wood screws and washers (8)

#10 x 1¼″ Flathead wood screws (72–84)

4 Swivel casters with brakes and mounting screws (4)

Making the Radial Arm Saw Stand

1 *Determine the dimensions.* The stand supports a radial arm saw at a comfortable height for woodworking. Measure the base of your saw to be sure it will fit on the stand. If the stand shown is too large or too small, make the appropriate changes in the plans and the Materials List. Also consider where you want the drawers and the shelf. As shown, the drawers are on the left and the shelf on the right. Switch this, if you want. You can also put drawers on both sides, or a shelf on both sides.

2 *Cut the parts.* Purchase 4/4 birch lumber (for the trim, stiles, rails, and drawer faces) and cabinet-grade birch veneer plywood (for everything else) to make the cabinet. Plane the solid stock ¾" thick. Then cut the parts for the case ("A" through "L" on the Materials List). Don't cut the door or drawer parts yet — there will be too many parts to keep track of.

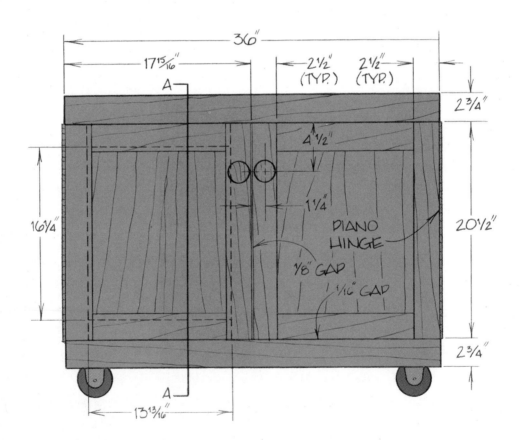

FRONT VIEW
(WITH DOORS IN PLACE)

3

Cut the rabbets, dadoes, and notches.
The plywood parts of the stand are assembled
with rabbets and dadoes. The braces are set in notches in
the divider. Here's a list of the cuts you must make:
- ¾"-wide, 2⅜"-long notches in the top edge of the
  divider to hold the braces
- ¾"-wide, ⅜"-deep rabbets in the back edges of
  the top and sides to hold the back
- ¾"-wide, ⅜"-deep rabbets in the top edges of the
  sides to hold the top
- ¾"-wide, ⅜"-deep dadoes in the sides to hold the
  bottom and the shelf

- ¾"-wide, ⅜"-deep dadoes in the divider to hold
  the shelf
- ¾"-wide, ⅜"-deep dadoes in the center of the top
  and bottom to hold the divider
- ¾"-wide, ¼"-deep dadoes in the left (or right)
  side and the divider to hold the drawer supports

Cut the notches with a saber saw. Make all the rabbets
and dadoes with a router, a straight bit, and the T-square
routing jig shown in the Routing chapter. Don't use a
dado cutter unless you want to cover all the areas to be
cut with masking tape. Otherwise, it will tear the veneer.

4

Assemble the case. To start, dry assemble
the top, bottom, sides, divider, and back to be
sure they fit. When you're satisfied they do, join the
bottom, sides, and divider with glue and flathead wood
screws. Counterbore and countersink each screw, then
cover the head with a wooden plug. Screw the top in
place, but *don't* glue it in place yet. You'll need to
remove it in just a little while. Secure the back to the
assembly, and let the glue set.

Remove the top, loosening the screws that hold it.
Glue the braces to the sides, and drive counterbored,
countersunk screws through the sides into them. Attach
the kicker between the front and middle braces (as
shown in the *Front View* and *Section A*). Replace the
top, gluing *and* screwing it to the case. Finally, attach the
front trim pieces. When the glue dries, sand the joints
and screw plugs clean and flush. Be careful not to sand
too deep; you might sand through the plywood's veneer.

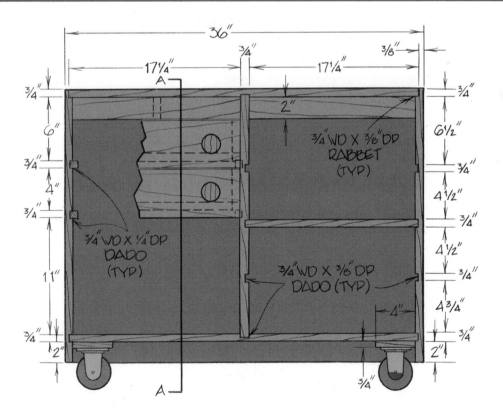

FRONT VIEW
(WITHOUT DOORS)

5

Install the drawer supports.   Glue the drawer supports inside the case, each in a ¾"-wide, ¼"-deep dado. Wedge them in place while the glue dries. To do this, cut pieces of scrap slightly longer than the distance between a set of supports — about 16". Place one end of the scrap against one support, then force the other end against the opposite support. After the glue dries, remove the scraps.

6

Install the casters.   Glue and screw the caster blocks to the bottom of the case. Place the casters on the blocks and check that each caster swivels freely, without hitting any part of the case. Drill pilot holes for the mounting screws, and secure the casters to the caster blocks.

7

Make the drawers.   Measure the inside of the case. Large projects have a way of changing dimension as you build them; you may have to adjust the sizes of the drawers somewhat. When you are sure of the dimensions, cut the drawer parts.

As the *Drawer/Side View* shows, each drawer front and back is joined to the sides with half-blind dovetails, and the bottom floats in grooves. Cut the grooves with a table-mounted router or a dado cutter, and the dovetails with a router and a dovetail jig. If you don't have this jig, use lock joints or rabbet joints instead of dovetails.

Assemble the front, back, and sides of each drawer with glue. Put the bottom in place when you put the drawer together, but don't glue it in the grooves. Let the glue dry, then sand the joints clean and flush.

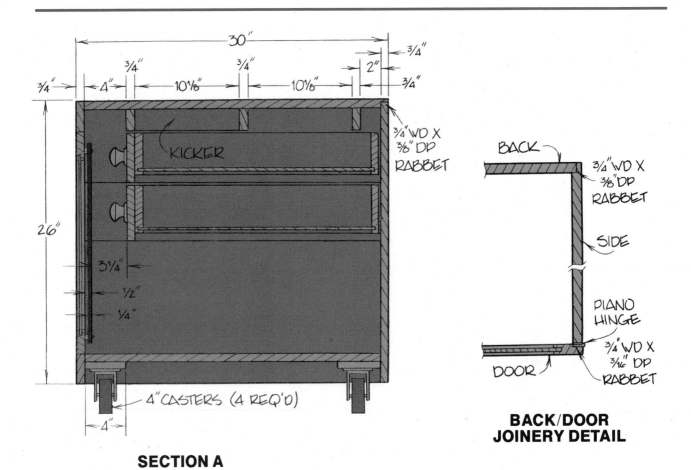

SECTION A

BACK/DOOR JOINERY DETAIL

8

Attach the drawer faces and pulls.
Place the drawers in the case and check that they slide in and out easily. If they bind, plane or sand the part that rubs.

Temporarily attach the drawer faces to the drawer fronts using double-faced carpet tape. Position the drawer faces so the gap between them is ⅛" wide. Mark the locations of the drawer pulls. Drill the holes for the mounting screws through the drawer faces *and* the drawer fronts.

Remove the faces and the tape. Spread glue on the drawer fronts, then attach the faces and the drawer pulls. Pass the mounting bolt for each pull through *both* the front and the face, so the bolt holds the two parts together. **Note:** The bolts that come with the pulls may not be long enough. If so, buy 2"-long bolts to fit the pulls.

9

Make the doors. The door parts are joined with tongue and groove joints. Tongues on the ends of the rails fit into grooves in the stiles. The panels float in grooves in both parts. The completed doors are installed with piano hinges, which fit in rabbets cut in the outside stiles. You can make all of these joints with a table-mounted router or a dado cutter.

Cut the recesses for the hinges first, making ¾"-wide, ³⁄₁₆"-deep rabbets down the inside faces of the outside stiles. Then cut ¼"-wide, ½"-deep grooves in the inside edges of the rails and stiles. Finally, form ¼"-wide, ½"-long tongues in the ends of the rails. To make each tongue, cut a rabbet across one end of the rail. Turn the rail over and cut a second rabbet in the same end, forming the tongue.

Assemble the doors, gluing the rails to the stiles. Don't glue the panels in the grooves; let them float. Let the glue dry, then sand the joints clean and flush.

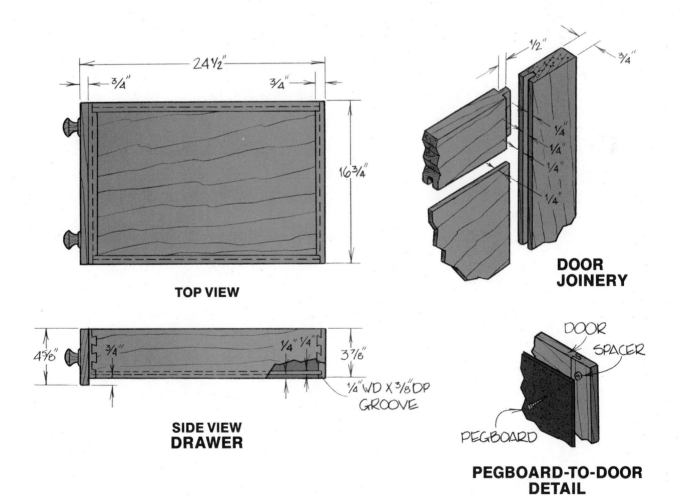

TOP VIEW

SIDE VIEW DRAWER

DOOR JOINERY

PEGBOARD-TO-DOOR DETAIL

10 Mount the doors on the cabinet.

Attach piano hinges to the backs of the doors, in the rabbets you have cut for them. Mount the doors on the cabinet, driving just the top and bottom screw on each hinge. Close both doors. The outside edges of the doors should be flush with the cabinet, and there should be a ⅛″ gap between the doors.

If the doors aren't aligned properly when closed, remove one (or more) of the *cabinet* hinge screws (not the screws in the door). Put a wooden matchstick or toothpick in the pilot hole to fill it, then move the screw right or left. When the doors are mounted properly, install the remainder of the screws. Attach catches and pulls.

Secure the pegboard panels to the backs of the doors. With a hacksaw, cut ½″-long spacers from ¼″ I.D. pipe. Drive a roundhead screw through each panel corner, slip the spacer on the screw, and drive the screw into the corner of the door. (Inset the edges of each panel about 1″ from the edges of the door.) The panel will be held away from the door so you can insert hooks in the pegboard.

11 Apply a finish and install the shelf.

Remove the doors, drawers, and all the hardware. Lightly sand the completed stand, then apply an oil finish. When the finish dries, apply paste wax. The oil and wax prevent glue from sticking to the wood, and keep the cabinet from getting stained and dirty.

Reassemble the cabinet, and slide the adjustable shelf into one set of dadoes.

Donut Chocks for Swivel Casters

Tools mounted on swivel casters may move or creep as you use them, even if you use casters with brakes. Ordinary wedge-shaped chocks won't solve this problem because the casters rotate. Instead, you must make donut-shaped chocks. Each wheel rests in the donut hole. Cut the hole with a hole saw, making it about 1″ *smaller* than the diameter of the caster wheel, so the caster can't roll or swivel.

To install and remove these chocks easily, make the simple lever-jack shown. Put the notched end of the jack under the cabinet or tool stand and pull back on the lever. As the tool rises up, slide the chock in or out of position. (See Figure A.)

A/Donut chocks keep casters from rolling and swiveling. Make them from plywood so they won't split or crack, and use a lever-jack to install and remove them.

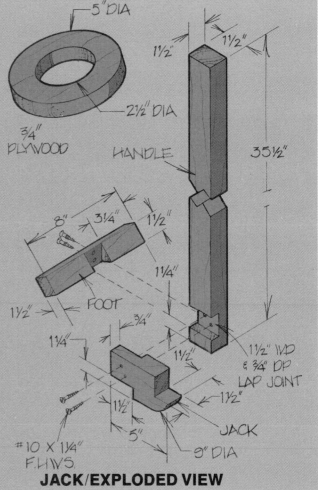

JACK/EXPLODED VIEW

Table Saw Shelves

Your table saw has two vital accessories, a miter gauge and a rip fence. You use them frequently, so you want to keep them handy.

The handiest place to keep them, perhaps, is right under the saw table — there's plenty of space beneath the table extensions. Most table saws have two extensions, one on the right, the other on the left. Under the right extension (as you face the infeed side of the table saw), you'll usually find the blade tilt crank. But the left extension has nothing under it. You can suspend several shelves there (*without* interfering with the saw's operation), using otherwise wasted space to store the miter gauge, rip fence, blades, dado cutter, and other accessories.

The unit shown has three shelves — two fixed and one sliding. The upper shelf holds the miter gauge, with room to spare for pushsticks and other small accessories. The middle shelf holds spare saw blades and slides out so you can reach them easily. The lower shelf holds the rip fence. Since the fence is longer than the shelving unit, the sides are cut out to create a cradle for it. Both fixed shelves have ledges along the front edges to keep the accessories from falling off. (Without them, the saw's vibration will cause the accessories to "walk" over the edges of the shelves.) The unit is attached to the saw housing and the extension table with screws.

Materials List

FINISHED DIMENSIONS

PARTS

A. Sides (2)   ¾" x (variable) x (variable)

B. Fixed shelves (2)   ¾" x (variable) x (variable)

C. Sliding shelf   ¾" x (variable) x (variable)

D. Ledges (2)   ¼" x 1" x (variable)

E. Trim (optional)   ¼" x ¾" x (variable)

F. Dowels (1–2)   ½" dia. x ¾"

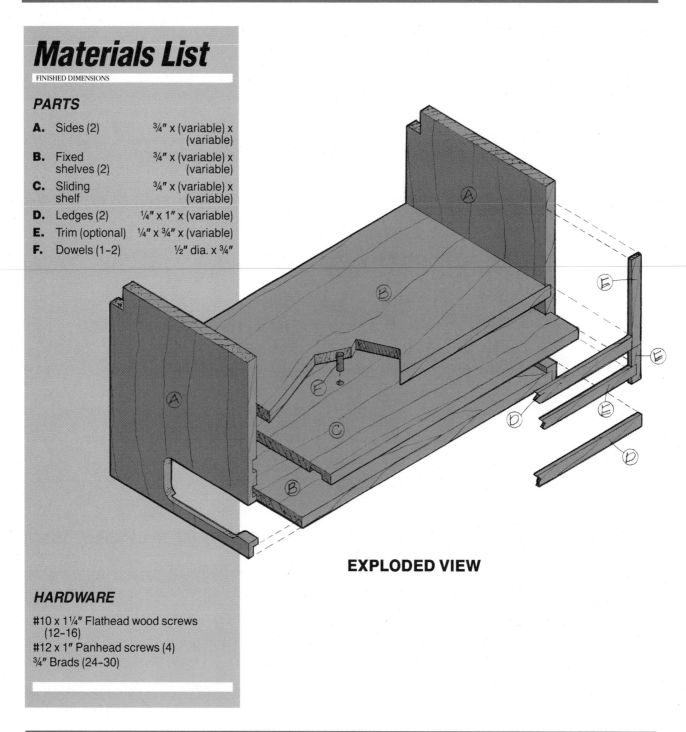

EXPLODED VIEW

HARDWARE

#10 x 1¼" Flathead wood screws (12–16)
#12 x 1" Panhead screws (4)
¾" Brads (24–30)

---

1 **Determine the dimensions.** You must tailor this shelving unit to your saw — the dimensions will be different for each make and model. To determine the unit's length, measure the metal saw housing from the infeed side to the outfeed side. (See Figure 1.) Don't make the shelves any longer than this housing. If the unit extends beyond it, you may have difficulty seeing and reaching the on/off switch.

To establish the depth of the shelves, measure from the side of the housing to the outboard edge of the left table extension. Subtract the width of the metal edge — usually about ⅛". For the height, measure from the bottom of the housing to the underside of the extension. Inspect the area under the extension for protrusions, and carefully measure them. (See Figure 2.) You will probably have to notch the sides of the shelving unit to accommodate saw table overhang, extension mounting bolts, or other hardware.

Finally, establish the shelf positions. Make the distance from the upper fixed shelf to the table extension equal to the height of the miter gauge plus ½″ (or more). The distance from the middle (sliding) shelf to the upper shelf should be ¾″ or more. Make the distance from the lower shelf to the middle shelf equal to the height of the rip fence plus ½″ (or more). If there isn't enough room for all three shelves, you may want to eliminate the sliding shelf.

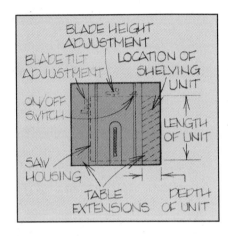

1/Make the shelving unit as long as the saw housing but no longer. When you mount the unit, position it flush with or slightly behind the front of the housing, so the shelves don't interfere with your access to the on/off switch.

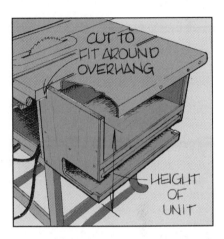

2/When you take measurements for the shelving unit, remember that its sides must butt against the underside of the extension, fitting between the inboard and outboard edges as shown. They must also fit around any protrusions.

2 Cut the parts.
Figure the variable dimensions on the Materials List and the drawings. Cross-check your measurements, then cut the parts from cabinet-grade plywood.

TRY THIS! To be certain the shelving unit will fit *before* you cut wood, draw a full-scale layout of the sides on poster board. Include all necessary notches and cutouts. Cut it out and test fit it to your saw.

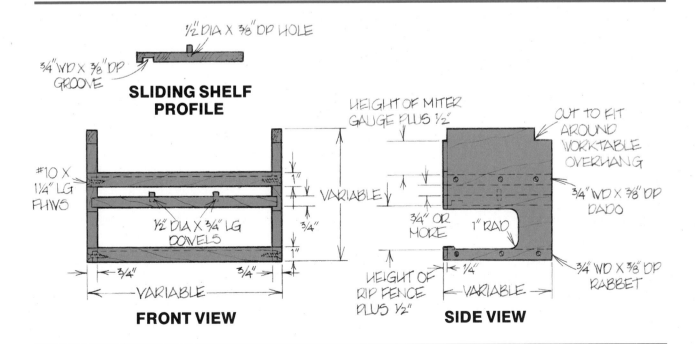

SLIDING SHELF PROFILE

FRONT VIEW

SIDE VIEW

3

Cut the joinery and the shapes of the sides. Lay out the dadoes, rabbets, notches, and cut-outs on the sides and sliding shelf. Make the dadoes and rabbets with a router or a dado cutter. Cut the notches and other shapes in the sides with a band saw or saber saw. Test fit the sides to the table saw. If they don't quite fit, trim a little off the depth or height, or enlarge the notches with a rasp.

4

Assemble the shelving unit. Test fit the shelves to the sides to be certain they fit. When you're satisfied they do, assemble the parts with glue and flathead wood screws. After the glue dries, sand the joints clean and flush.

5

Mount the shelving unit to the table saw. Since you will be working inside your table saw during this step, avoid injury by unplugging it and removing the blade from the arbor.

Drill ³⁄₁₆″-diameter holes in the saw housing and the edge of the left table extension. (See Figure 3.) Fit the shelving assembly in place. Drive panhead screws through the housing and extension into the wooden sides.

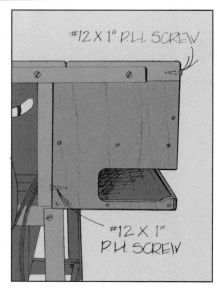

3/Attach the shelving unit with four screws — two through the edge of the extension and two through the housing, as shown. Be careful when you drive the screws from inside the housing. To prevent injury, unplug the saw and remove the blade from the arbor.

6

Install the sliding shelf in the assembly. With the unit mounted on the saw, test fit the sliding shelf to the assembly. If it binds in the dadoes, trim a little off the length. Drill ½″-diameter, ⅜″-deep holes for the dowels that will hold the saw blades. Glue the dowels in the holes.

7

Attach the ledges and the trim. Glue the ledges to the front edges of the fixed shelves, tacking them in place with brads. The bottom edge of each ledge should be flush with the bottom surface of the shelf, so the top edge of the ledge protrudes ¼″ above the shelf.

Trim the exposed plywood edges to hide the plies. Notch this trim to fit around the dado for the sliding shelf. Then attach it with glue and brads, in the same manner as the ledges.

Tool Cabinet

In every workshop, a particular assortment of tools and materials is used frequently — favorite hand tools, oft-needed portable power tools, measuring and marking gauges, glues, sandpaper, and so on. In an efficient shop, these items should be stored close to each other, near the work.

The tool cabinet lets you store these things in one place. It has shelves, drawers, and hanging storage, so you can store a variety of workshop items. When you're working, it opens up to display your tools and make them easy to reach. Although it's a large cabinet, it rolls easily on casters, letting you position your tools close to your work. Set the brakes on the casters, and the cabinet will stay where you put it.

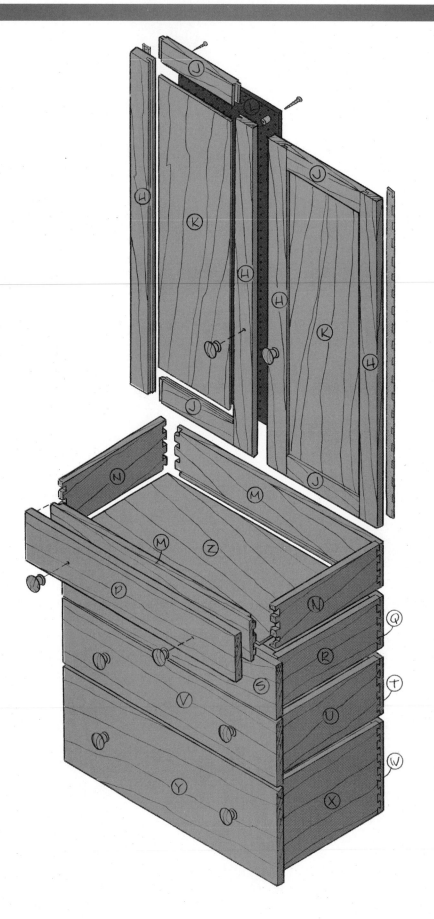

EXPLODED VIEW

Materials List

FINISHED DIMENSIONS

PARTS

A. Top   ¾" x 15¼" x 29¼"

B. Middle shelf/
bottom (2)   ¾" x 15" x 29¼"

C. Sides (2)   ¾" x 15¼" x 74"

D. Back   ¼" x 29¼" x 73⅝"

E. Front trim   ¾" x 2¾" x 30"

F. Caster blocks (4)   ¾" x 4" x 4"

G. Adjustable
shelves (2-3)   ¾" x 11" x 29⅛"

H. Door stiles (4)   ¾" x 2½" x 38"

J. Door rails (4)   ¾" x 2½" x 10¹⁵/₁₆"

K. Door panels (2)   ¼" x 10¹³/₁₆" x 33⅞"

L. Pegboard panels (2)   ¼" x 13" x 36"

M. Top drawer
front/back (2)   ¾" x 5⅛" x 28⅜"

N. Top drawer
sides (2)   ¾" x 5⅛" x 14¼"

P. Top drawer face   ¾" x 5⅞" x 30"

Q. Upper middle drawer
front/back (2)   ¾" x 6⅛" x 28⅜"

R. Upper middle
drawer sides (2)   ¾" x 6⅛" x 14¼"

S. Upper middle
drawer face   ¾" x 6⅞" x 30"

T. Lower middle drawer
front/back (2)   ¾" x 7⅛" x 28⅜"

U. Lower middle
drawer sides (2)   ¾" x 7⅛" x 14¼"

V. Lower middle
drawer face   ¾" x 7⅞" x 30"

W. Bottom drawer
front/back (2)   ¾" x 11⅜" x 28⅜"

X. Bottom drawer
sides (2)   ¾" x 11⅜" x 14¼"

Y. Bottom
drawer face   ¾" x 12" x 30"

Z. Drawer
bottoms (4)   ¼" x 14¼" x 27⅝"

HARDWARE

1½" x 38" Piano hinges and mounting
screws (1 pair)

2" Door/drawer pulls (10)

Cabinet door catches (2)

#12 x 1½" Roundhead wood screws
and flat washers (8)

¼" I.D. Pipe (5"-6")

#10 x 1¼" Flathead wood screws
(24-30)

1" Brads (30-40)

4" Swivel casters with brakes and
mounting screws (4)

1

Determine the dimensions. As designed, the tool cabinet will hold a large assortment of hand and portable power tools. The shelves are adjustable; the dadoes in the upper portion of the cabinet let you arrange either three or four shelves with different spacing between them. (See Figures 1 and 2.)

However, you may have special storage needs. Consider the size and the amount of the things that you want to put in this cabinet. Do you need more shelves? Or do you need fewer drawers? Should the spacing between the shelves be different? Should the drawers be deeper or more shallow? Decide on an arrangement that will suit you, then make the appropriate changes in the plans and the Materials List.

1/If you have a lot of large objects to store in the cabinet, arrange the upper portion so you have three widely spaced shelves.

2/If you have a variety of large and small items, arrange the upper portion so you have four shelves with wide, medium, and narrow spaces between them.

2

Cut the parts. Purchase 4/4 birch lumber (for the trim, stiles, rails, and drawer faces) and cabinet-grade birch veneer plywood (for everything else) to make the cabinet. Plane the solid stock ¾″ thick. Then cut the parts for the case ("A" through "G" on the Materials List). Don't cut the door or drawer parts yet — there will be too many parts to keep track of.

3

Cut the rabbets and dadoes. Assemble the cabinet case with rabbets and dadoes. Here's a list of the cuts you must make:

- ¾″-wide, ⅜″-deep rabbets in the top edges of the sides to hold the top
- ¾″-wide, ⅜″-deep dadoes in the sides to hold the bottom and the shelves
- ¾″-wide, ¼″-deep dadoes in the sides to hold the drawer supports
- ¼″-wide, ⅜″-deep rabbets in the back edges of the top and sides to hold the back

Make all the joints with a router, a straight bit, and the T-square routing jig shown in the Routing chapter. (See Figure 3.) Don't use a dado cutter; it will tear the veneer.

3/Carefully measure and mark the positions of the dadoes and rabbets. Line up the T-square jig with each mark, clamp it to the workpiece, and rout the joint. Make each joint in several passes, routing ⅛″–¼″ deeper with each pass.

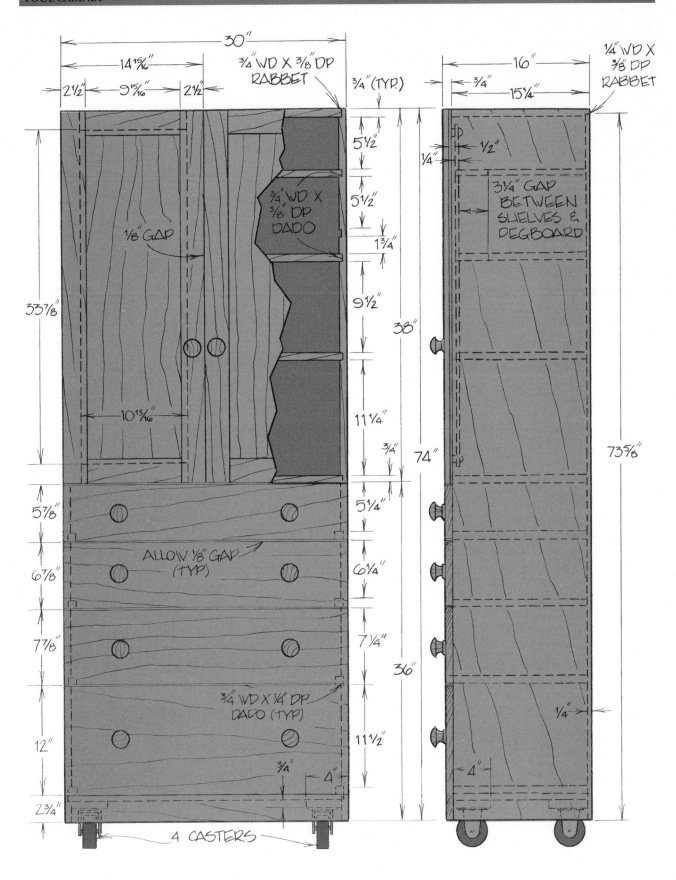

FRONT VIEW   **SIDE VIEW**

4 **Assemble the case.** To start, dry assemble the top, bottom, sides, middle shelf, and back to be sure they fit. When you're satisfied they do, join the top, bottom, middle shelf, and sides with glue and flat-head wood screws. Counterbore and countersink each screw, then cover the head with a wooden plug. Attach the back to the assembly with glue and brads, then let the glue set.

Attach the front trim flush with the bottom of the assembly. When the glue dries, sand all joints and screw plugs clean and flush. Be careful not to sand too deep; you might sand through the plywood's veneer.

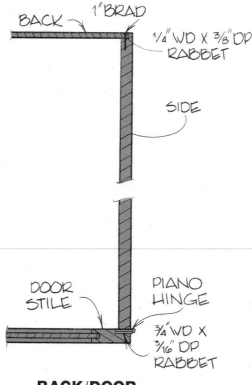

BACK
1" BRAD
¼" WD X ⅜" DP RABBET
SIDE
DOOR STILE
PIANO HINGE
¾" WD X ³⁄₁₆" DP RABBET

**BACK/DOOR
JOINERY DETAIL**

5 **Install the drawer supports.** Glue the drawer supports inside the case, each in a ¾"-wide, ¼"-deep dado. Wedge them in place while the glue dries. To do this, cut pieces of scrap slightly longer than the distance between a set of supports — about 27⅝". Place one end of the scrap against one support, then force the other end against the opposite support. (See Figure 4.) After the glue dries, remove the scraps.

4/Wedge the supports to the sides while the glue dries. Use at least three wedges for each support — one at each end and one in the middle.

6 **Install the casters.** Glue and screw the caster blocks to the bottom of the case. Place the casters on the blocks and check that each caster swivels freely, without hitting any part of the case. Drill pilot holes for the mounting screws, and secure the casters to the caster blocks.

7

Make the drawers. Measure the inside of the case. Large projects have a way of changing dimension as you build them; you may have to adjust the sizes of the drawers somewhat. When you are sure of the dimensions, cut the drawer parts.

As the *Drawer/Side View* shows, each drawer front and back is joined to the sides with half-blind dovetails, and the bottom floats in grooves. Cut the grooves with a table-mounted router or a dado cutter, and the dovetails with a router and a dovetail jig. If you don't have this jig, use lock joints or rabbet joints instead of dovetails. (See Figure 5.)

Assemble the front, back, and sides of each drawer with glue. Put the bottom in place when you put the drawer together, but don't glue it in the grooves. Let the glue dry, then sand the joints clean and flush.

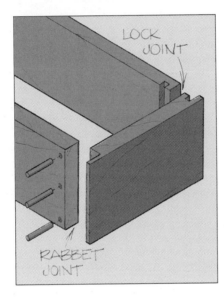

5/If you don't have a jig to make dovetails — and don't want to make them by hand — use lock joints or rabbet joints. Either joint can be made with a router, a dado cutter, or a saw. If you use rabbets, reinforce the joints with dowels.

TOP VIEW

SIDE VIEW DRAWER

8

Attach the drawer faces and pulls. Place the drawers in the case and check that they slide in and out easily. If they bind, plane or sand the part that rubs.

Arrange the drawer faces over the drawers, using bar clamps to hold them against the edges of the case. Adjust their positions so the spacing between them is even. There should be a ⅛" gap between adjacent faces, and the ends of each face should be flush with the case sides.

When the faces are properly positioned, mark the locations of the drawer pulls. Drill the holes for the mounting screws through the drawer faces *and* the drawer fronts. (See Figure 6.)

Remove the clamps and the faces. Spread glue on the drawer fronts, then attach the faces and the drawer pulls. Pass the mounting bolt for each pull through *both* the front and the face, so the bolt holds the two parts

6/With the faces clamped over the drawer assemblies, drill holes to mount the drawer pulls. Each hole must pass through **both** the drawer face and front. When you install the pulls, the mounting bolts will hold the faces in place.

together. **Note:** The bolts that come with the pulls may not be long enough. If so, purchase 2"-long bolts to fit the pulls.

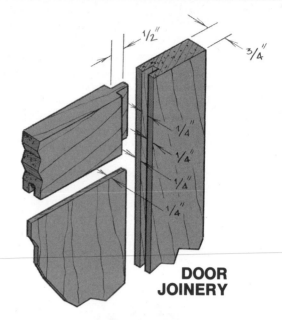

9

Make the doors.   The door parts are joined with tongue and groove joints. Tongues on the ends of the rails fit into grooves in the stiles. The panels float in grooves in both parts. The completed doors are installed with piano hinges, which fit in rabbets cut in the outside stiles. Make all of these joints with a table-mounted router or a dado cutter.

Cut the recesses for the hinges first, making ¾"-wide, ³⁄₁₆"-deep rabbets down the inside faces of the outside stiles. Then cut ¼"-wide, ½"-deep grooves in the inside edges of the rails and stiles. (See Figure 7.) Finally, form ¼"-wide, ½"-long tongues in the ends of the rails. To make each tongue, cut a rabbet across one end of the rail. Turn the rail over and cut a second rabbet in the same end, forming the tongue. (See Figure 8.)

Assemble the doors, gluing the rails to the stiles. Don't glue the panels in the grooves; let them float. Let the glue dry, then sand the joints clean and flush.

DOOR JOINERY

*7/Cut a groove in the **inside** edge of each door part. Center this groove **precisely** in the edge.*

8/To make a tongue, cut two rabbets in the end of a board — one in each face. Attach a stop block to the fence to gauge the length of the tongue and prevent kickback.

10

Mount the doors on the cabinet.
Attach piano hinges to the backs of the doors, in the rabbets you have cut for them. Mount the doors on the cabinet, driving just the top and bottom screw on each hinge. Close both doors. The outside edges of the doors should be flush with the cabinet, and there should be a ⅛" gap between the doors.

If the doors aren't aligned properly when closed, remove one (or more) of the *cabinet* hinge screws (not the screws in the doors). Put a wooden matchstick or toothpick in the pilot hole to fill it, then move the screw right or left. When the doors are mounted properly, install the remainder of the screws. Attach catches and pulls.

Secure the pegboard panels to the backs of the doors. With a hacksaw, cut ½"-long spacers from ¼" I.D. pipe. Drive a roundhead screw through each panel corner, slip the spacer on the screw, and drive the screw into the cor-

ner of the door. (Inset the edges of each panel about 1" from the edges of the door.) The panel will be held away from the door so you can insert hooks in the pegboard.

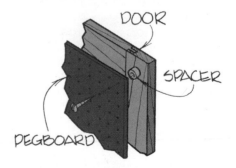

PEGBOARD-TO-DOOR DETAIL

11 *Apply a finish and install the shelves.*

Remove the doors, drawers, and all the hardware. Lightly sand the completed cabinet, then apply an oil finish. When the finish dries, apply paste wax. The oil and wax prevent glue from sticking to the wood, and helps keep the cabinet from getting stained and dirty.

Reassemble the cabinet, and slide the adjustable shelves into the dadoes.

Wood Rack

Wood presents perplexing storage problems. Its shape — long and narrow — is inconvenient. A first instinct is to store it standing on end, leaning against a wall. But if you leave the boards like this for very long, they may warp. You can't lay them down on the floor; you'll trip over them.

The best solution is to build a wood rack. It doesn't have to occupy a lot of space. The rack shown stores 60-75 board feet of lumber in just 8-12 square feet. It's inexpensive; you build it from construction grade 2 x 4. And it's easy to make. Simply nail it together and bolt it to one wall of your shop.

Materials List

FINISHED DIMENSIONS

PARTS

A. Uprights
(variable)   1½" x 3½" x (variable)
B. Ledges (variable)   1½" x 3½" x 12"
C. Brace (variable)   1½" x 3½" x 16"

HARDWARE

16d Common nails (variable)
⅜" x 5" Lag bolts (variable)
⅜" Flat washers (variable)

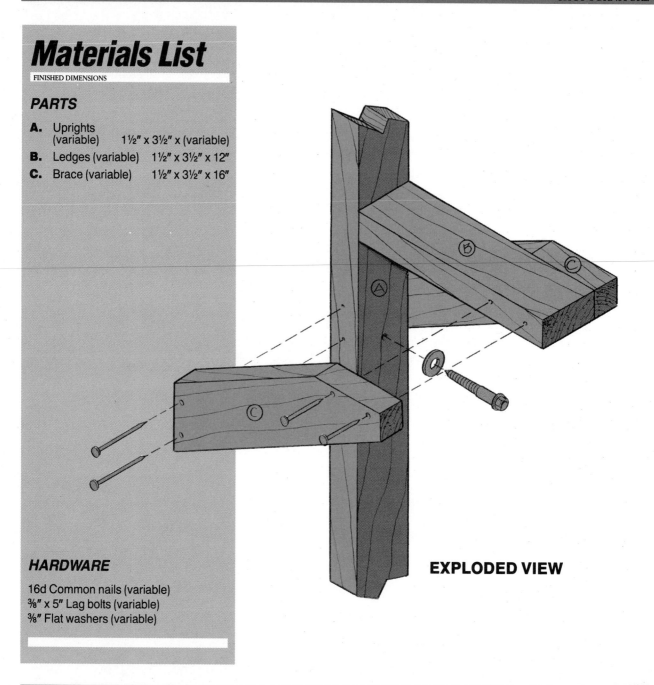

EXPLODED VIEW

1 Determine the location and the configuration.

Consider where you will put the rack. This, more than anything else, will determine how large you make it. When you have selected a wall, locate the studs in it. Each upright must be attached to a stud for the rack to support the wood. The number and the spacing of the studs in the wall will determine how many uprights you must cut and how you will space them.

If the wall is made from concrete or masonry, you can attach uprights almost anywhere you want. The drawback is that it's more difficult to attach them.

Measure the distance from floor to ceiling — this will determine the length of the uprights. Look for obstructions; you may have to cut some uprights shorter than others. Consider the placement of your tools, windows, doors, outlets, and switches. These things will determine how many ledges there will be and where to locate them. For example, the wood rack shown only has three ledges on each upright, all placed high above the floor. This keeps the outlets clear, and yields a place for a workbench or power tool.

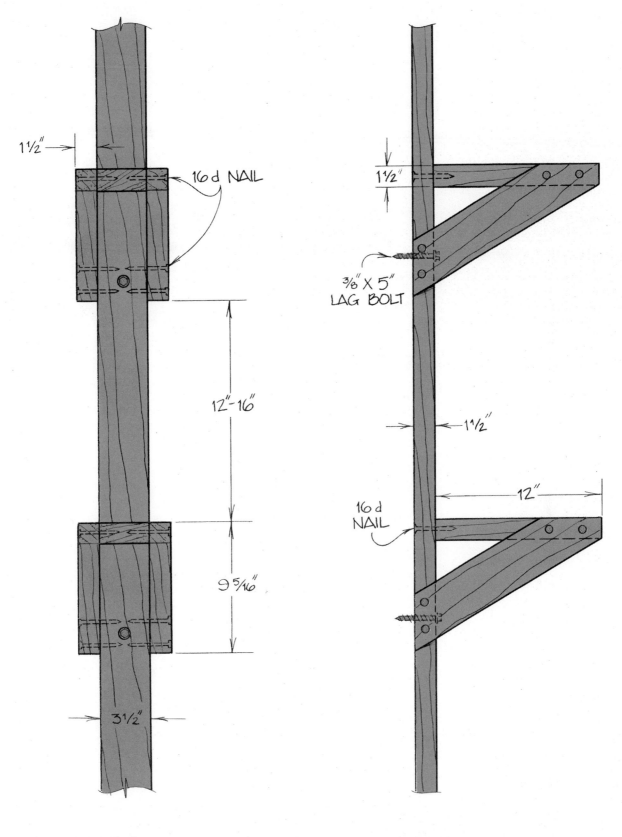

1½"

16d NAIL

12"–16"

9 5/16"

3½"

1½"

3/8" X 5"
LAG BOLT

1½"

12"

16d
NAIL

FRONT VIEW   **SIDE VIEW**

2

Cut the parts. When you have decided where to put the rack and how to build it, cut the parts. Miter the ends of the brace, as shown in the *Brace Layout*. Notice that the ends of the braces have parallel miters, and that *one* end of each brace is double-mitered. Adjust the miter gauge to 60°, and cut the braces to length, mitering *both* ends. Be sure you make the cuts parallel. (See Figure 1.) Readjust the angle of the miter gauge to 30°, and attach a miter gauge extension. (See Figure 2.) Cut a 30° miter in one end of each brace.

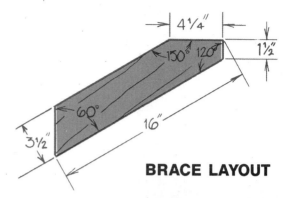

BRACE LAYOUT

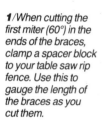

1/When cutting the first miter (60°) in the ends of the braces, clamp a spacer block to your table saw rip fence. Use this to gauge the length of the braces as you cut them.

*2/Clamp or screw a stop block to the miter gauge extension to position the braces on the saw for the second miter (30°). Double-miter just **one** end of each brace.*

3

Assemble the rack. Nail one end of the ledgers to the uprights. Position the braces, and nail these to both the uprights and the ledgers, as shown in the *Side View.*

4

Attach the rack assemblies to the wall. If you're installing the rack on a frame wall, mark the positions of the studs. If you have trouble finding the studs, use this trick:

Tap on the wall with a hammer until the pitch of the tap rises slightly and sounds less hollow. Drill a ¼″ hole in the wall at this point; if you're over a stud, you'll see sawdust coming out of the hole as you drill it. If you don't hit a stud, make a feeler gauge by bending a right angle in the middle of a 6″-long coat-hanger wire. Insert one half of the wire *and* the bend in the hole. Let the bent part hang straight down, then turn it right or left. If you're near the stud, the wire will hit it. (See Figure 3.) This will tell you in which direction the stud lies, and about how far away it is. Try again, drilling another hole.

Tack the rack assemblies in place over the studs with 16d nails. One by one, remove the nails, drill pilot holes, and drive lag bolts through the uprights into the studs.

If you're installing the rack on a concrete or masonry wall, drill pilot holes in the uprights first. Have a helper

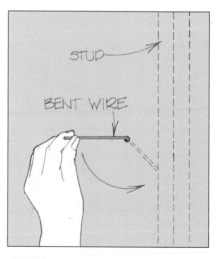

3/If you don't find the stud when you drill the hole, feel for it with a bent wire. If you're near the stud, the wire will hit it. You can sense where the stud is from the direction in which you turn the wire and how far you turn it.

hold each upright in place on the wall and mark the positions of the holes. Using a masonry bit, drill ½″-diameter, 3″-deep holes for expansion shields. Insert the shields in the wall, put the racks in place, and drive lag bolts through the upright and into the shields.

Sawing Tools

- **Long-and-Strong Fence Extension**
- **Miter Gauge Extensions**
- **Self-Cleaning Radial Arm Saw Backstop**
- **Tapering Jig**
- **Resawing Fence**
- **Fretwork Table**

As capable as the saws in your shop may seem, most of them are designed to handle only common sawing tasks. If a cut is out of the ordinary, you may need a sawing jig or fixture to make it safely and accurately.

The shopmade jigs shown increase the versatility of your saws, allowing you to perform many special sawing jobs. They will also improve the ease and accuracy of some common chores. The *long-and-strong fence extension* aids in ripping long or large workpieces on your table saw. *Miter gauge extensions* hold large and specially-shaped stock at an angle to the table saw blade. The *self-cleaning radial arm saw backstop* does a better job of keeping a workpiece at the proper angle to a blade than ordinary radial arm saw fences. Its adjustable stop simplifies the cutting of duplicate lengths. The *tapering jig* controls long, angled cuts on either the table saw or radial arm saw. The *resawing fence* lets you cut stock to a specific thickness on the band saw, saving time and lumber. Finally, the *fretwork table* holds small-to-medium sized workpieces while you make intricate cuts with a coping saw, fretsaw, or jeweler's saw. Together with your saws, they will handle most sawing operations — common *and* not-so-common. ❋

Long-and-Strong Fence Extension

Large, long workpieces are difficult to control on the table saw, particularly at the end of a cut. As you finish feeding a board past the blade, most of it hangs over the outfeed edge of the saw table. The weight of the board drags it down; you have to exert enormous pressure to keep the wood on the table long enough to cut the last few inches. This part of the cut is likely wasted effort anyway. Since the rip fence doesn't extend past the saw table, there is little to control the sideways motion of the board. If the wood moves to the right or left as you finish cutting, the last portion of the cut will be inaccurate.

The long-and-strong fence extension solves both of these problems. It attaches to the rip fence, providing an additional 12″ to 15″ of support *and* guidance on the outfeed side of the saw table.

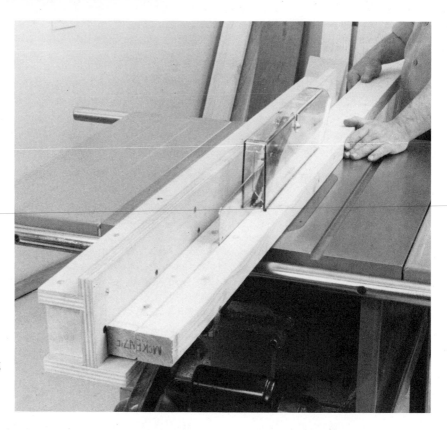

Materials List

FINISHED DIMENSIONS

PARTS

A. Fence extension   ¾″ x 4½″ x 48″
B. Brace   ¾″ x 2½″ x 48″
C. Ledge   ¾″ x 4½″ x (variable)
D. Support blocks (3)   ¾″ x 2¼″ x (variable)

HARDWARE

#10 x 1¼″ Flathead wood screws (18–20)
³⁄₁₆″ x 3″ Carriage bolts*, flat washers, and wing nuts (3–4)

The size and length of the carriage bolts may change depending on the make of your table saw.

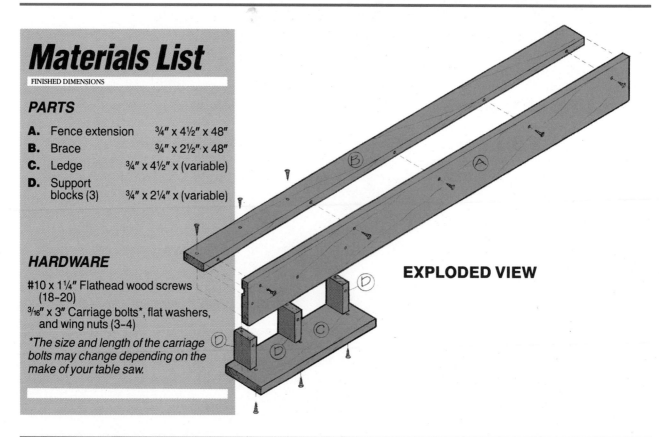

EXPLODED VIEW

1

Determine the dimensions.   Several of the dimensions on the plans are marked "variable." These are determined by the dimensions of your saw. Calculate the length of the ledge first.

The fence extension is 48″ long. The one shown is mounted on a saw with a table depth of 30″. The rear guide rail protrudes a little less than 2″ from the outfeed edge of the saw table. The ledge is 16″ long.

To fit the fence extension to your saw, measure the depth of the saw table (front to back). Note any castings or protrusions that could interfere with the fence extension — a mounting bracket for the saw guard, the guide rail for the rip fence, a pulley guard on the motor, and so on. Add the width of any such protrusions to the depth of the saw table, and subtract that sum from the length of the fence extension. The remainder will be the length of the ledge.

Determine where to position the brace next. The fence extension is 4½″ high. The one shown is mounted on a rip fence that is 2¾″ high, so the brace attaches to the extension 3″ from the bottom edge. The blocks that stabilize the ledge are 3″ long.

To determine what these dimensions will be for your saw, measure the height of the rip fence and add ¼″. The sum will be both the measurement from the bottom edge of the extension to the brace and the height of the blocks.

When you have figured these dimensions, cut all the parts.

2

Drill the bolt holes.   All table saw rip fences have holes to mount jigs, but the hole spacing is different from saw to saw. To mark the location of the carriage bolt holes on the extension, use your rip fence as a template. With the fence on the table saw, place the extension against the *right* side (the side facing away from the blade). Make sure the extension rests on the table surface, and the front edge is flush with the front edge of the rip fence. Stick an awl or a pencil through the holes in the fence, marking the extension.

Check the diameter of the holes in the fence. Most are ³⁄₁₆″, but yours may be different. At each mark, drill a ⅝″-diameter, ¼″-deep counterbore, then a smaller hole (the same diameter as the holes in the fence) through the extension.

3

Cut the groove in the extension.   Mark the extension where you will mount the brace. Using a router or a dado cutter, plow a ¾″-wide, ¼″-deep groove at this mark.

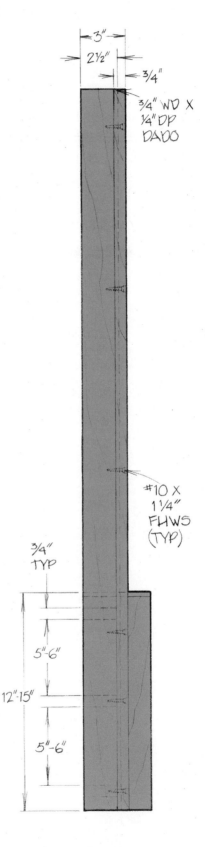

3″

2½″

¾″

¾″ WD X ¼″ DP DADO

#10 X 1¼″ FHWS (TYP)

¾″ TYP

5″-6″

12″-15″

5″-6″

TOP VIEW

4

Assemble and attach the fence extension. Glue the brace to the extension, and reinforce the joint with screws. Glue and screw the support blocks, then the ledge, to the assembly. Countersink all screws, especially those on the face of the extension, so they won't catch on a workpiece.

Position the extension against the *left* side of the rip fence (between the fence and the blade). Insert carriage bolts through the holes in the extension and secure it to the rip fence with washers and wing nuts. When you turn the nuts tight, the heads of the carriage bolts should be below the face of the extension.

5

Chamfer the infeed edge of the ledge. When attached to the rip fence, the ledge may sit slightly higher than the surface of the worktable — even though you were careful to build it at the same level. This is normal; a tiny amount of play in the mounting holes causes it. But it can be a *hazard!* A workpiece may catch on the ledge while you're cutting. If you continue to push, the stock may twist on the table and kick back.

To prevent this, chisel a small chamfer on the front (infeed) edge of the ledge. (See Figure 1.) This will be a ramp, lifting the workpiece up and over the edge.

*1/*To prevent a workpiece from catching on the ledge, chamfer the front edge. Then, to make sure the wood will feed properly, pass a board over the table and the ledge without the saw running. Do this test **before** you use the fence extension to cut stock.

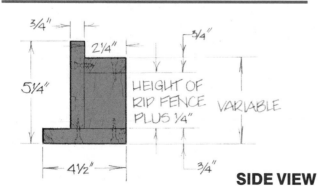

3/4"
2¼"
5¼"
4½"
3/4"
3/4"
HEIGHT OF RIP FENCE PLUS ¼" VARIABLE

SIDE VIEW

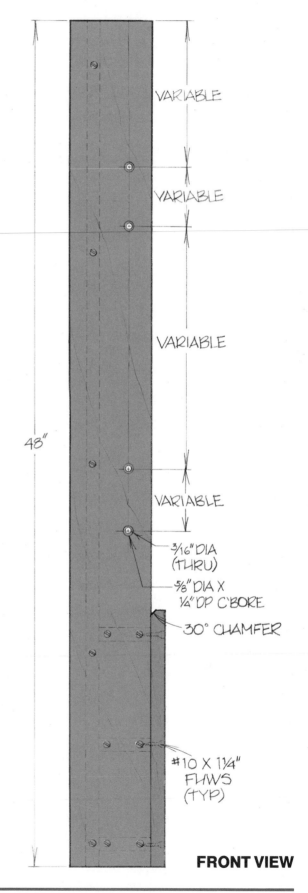

VARIABLE

VARIABLE

VARIABLE

48"

VARIABLE

3/16" DIA (THRU)

5/8" DIA X ¼" DP C'BORE

30° CHAMFER

#10 X 1¼" FHWS (TYP)

FRONT VIEW

Miter Gauge Extensions

The faces of most miter gauges are about 6″ long so you can use them on either side of the saw blade. This is hardly long enough, however, to provide adequate support when crosscutting or mitering. You need to attach an extension to your miter gauge to have it function with any accuracy.

The three extensions shown will help with a variety of sawing tasks. The *miter gauge extension* is for everyday woodworking. It simply extends the miter gauge face, so you have a longer surface to guide the stock. The *miter gauge cut-off extension* is much longer. The adjustable stop lets you duplicate small to medium-sized workpieces. The *miter gauge V-jig extension* supports and guides non-rectangular workpieces such as dowels and moldings. All these fixtures are reversible; that is, you can mount them so they extend from either side of the miter gauge. You can use them on either side of the saw blade.

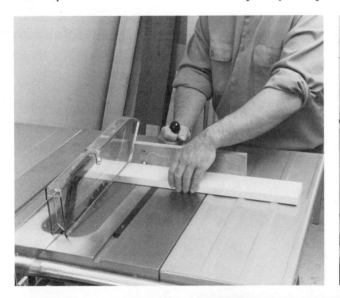

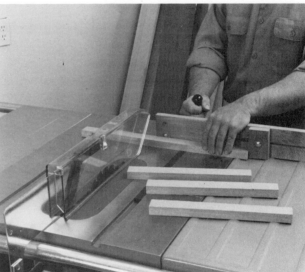

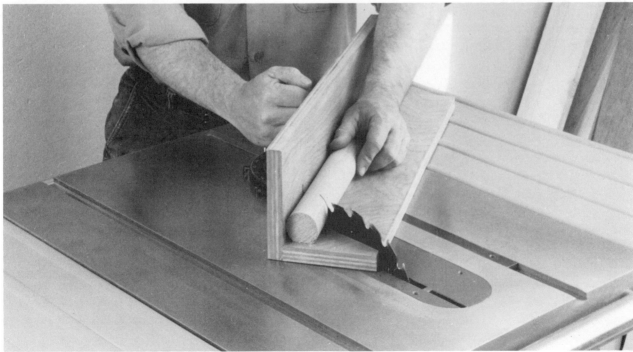

Materials List

FINISHED DIMENSIONS

PARTS

Miter Gauge Extension

A. Extension   ¾" x 3" x 12"

Miter Gauge Cut-Off Extension

A. Extension   ¾" x 3" x 24"
B. Stop   ¾" x 2" x 3"

Miter Gauge V-Jig Extension

A. Extension   ¾" x 5¼" x 24"
B. Base   ¾" x 4½" x 24"

HARDWARE

Miter Gauge Extension

³⁄₁₆" x 2½" Carriage bolts*, washers, and wing nuts (2)

Miter Gauge Cut-Off Extension

³⁄₁₆" x 2½" Carriage bolts*, washers, and wing nuts (2)
⅜" X 2¼" Carriage bolt, washer, and wing nut

Miter Gauge V-Jig Extension

#12 x 1¼" Roundhead wood screws* and washers (2)
#10 x 1¼" Brass flathead wood screws (4–6)

The diameter and length of these bolts and screws may change depending on the make of your table saw and miter gauge.

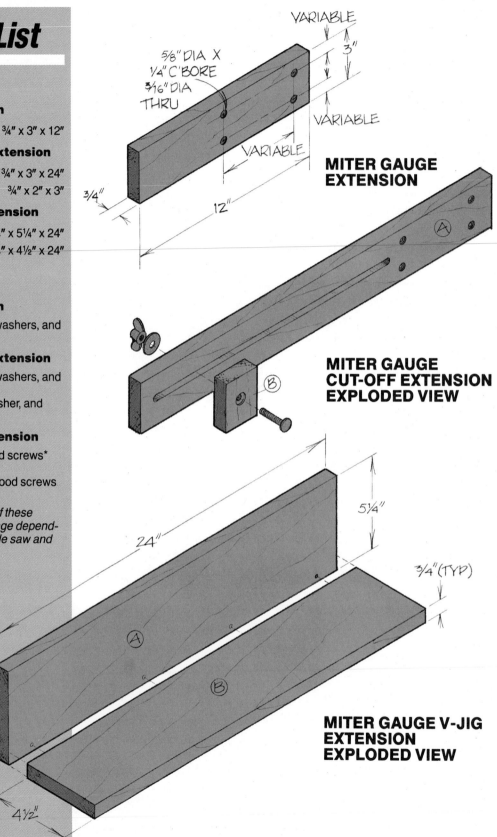

VARIABLE

5⁄8" DIA X
1⁄4" C'BORE
3⁄16" DIA
THRU

3"

VARIABLE

VARIABLE

3/4"

12"

MITER GAUGE EXTENSION

MITER GAUGE CUT-OFF EXTENSION EXPLODED VIEW

24"

5¼"

3/4" (TYP)

#10 X 1½"
FHWS
(4 REQ'D)

4½"

MITER GAUGE V-JIG EXTENSION EXPLODED VIEW

Making the Miter Gauge Extension

1 **Cut the part.**   Determine how long and how high you want to make the miter gauge extension. A good *all-purpose* size is 3″ x 12″, but you may have special applications. Some woodworkers make several extensions, each a different length and height. They choose the best size for each job. When you know what size you want, cut the part.

2 **Drill the holes.**   All table saw miter gauges have holes to mount extensions, but the hole spacing is different from gauge to gauge. To mark the location of the carriage bolt holes on the extension, use your miter gauge as a template. With the gauge in a table saw slot, place the extension against the face so the right sides of both the extension and the gauge are flush. Stick an awl or a pencil through the holes in the gauge and mark them on the extension.

Turn the extension over, switching the left and right ends. Place it against the face of the miter gauge with the left sides flush and mark a second set of holes. This will allow you to mount the extension so it extends from either the left or the right side of the gauge, making it reversible.

Check the diameter of the holes in the gauge. Most are ³/₁₆″, but yours may be different. At each of the marks, drill a ⅝″-diameter, ¼″-deep counterbore, then a smaller hole (the same diameter as the gauge holes) through the extension.

Note: On some makes, it's easier to attach a miter gauge extension with screws.

3 **Attach the extension.**   Insert carriage bolts through the holes in the extension. Secure it to the miter gauge with washers and wing nuts. When you turn the nuts tight, the heads of the carriage bolts should be below the face of the extension.

Making the Miter Gauge Cut-Off Extension

1 **Cut the parts.**   Decide whether the length of the extension shown will work well for you. You may want something slightly longer. (Don't make the extension too long. Over 36″, it is awkward.) When you have determined the length, cut the parts.

2 **Drill the holes.**   Use your miter gauge as a template to mark the location of the carriage bolt holes on the extension. With the gauge in a table saw slot, place the extension against the face so the right sides of both the extension and the gauge are flush. Stick an awl or a pencil through the holes in the gauge and mark them on the extension.

Turn the extension over, switching the left and right ends. Place it against the face of the miter gauge with the left sides flush and mark a second set of holes. This will allow you to mount the extension so it extends from either the left or the right side of the gauge, making it reversible.

Check the diameter of the holes in the gauge. Most are ³/₁₆″, but yours may be different. At each of the marks, drill a ⅝″-diameter, ¼″-deep counterbore, then a smaller hole (the same diameter as the gauge holes) through the extension.

Drill the bolt hole in the stop in a similar manner. Make a ¾″-diameter, ¼″-deep counterbore centered on the stop's face, then drill a ⅜″ hole through the stop.

Note: On some makes, it's easier to attach a miter gauge extension with screws.

3 **Cut the slot.** Lay out a ⁷/₁₆″-wide slot on the extension as shown in the *Front View.* If you're making the extension longer (or shorter) than shown, change the length of the slot to fit the extension. Drill a ⁷/₁₆″-diameter hole at each end, then cut the slot from hole to hole with a saber saw. (See Figure 1.) File the inside edges of the slot smooth.

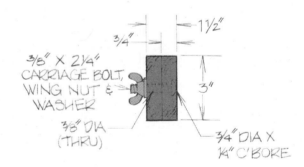

1/Cut the slot in the extension with a saber saw. Use a fine-tooth blade (10–20 teeth per inch). This will cut slower, but it will leave a smoother edge and you'll have less clean-up work to do.

SIDE VIEW

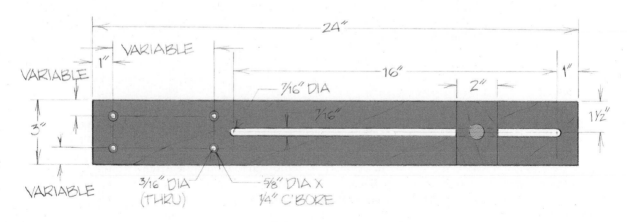

FRONT VIEW

4. Assemble and attach the extension.

Insert the ⅜″ carriage bolt through the hole in the stop, then secure it to the extension with a flat washer and wing nut. Insert the smaller bolts in the holes in the extension. Secure the extension assembly to the miter gauge with washers and wing nuts. When you turn the nuts tight, the heads of all carriage bolts — in the stop and in the extension — should be below the surface of the wood.

Making the Miter Gauge V-Jig Extension

1. Cut the parts.

Decide whether the length, depth, and height of the extension shown will work for you. You may want something different. (Some woodworkers make several V-jig extensions, each a different size so they can choose the best one for the job.) When you have determined the size you need, cut the parts.

2. Assemble the parts.

Glue the extension to the base, and reinforce the joint with *brass* wood screws. Brass is a soft metal. If you cut through the extension for any reason, the brass screws will not hurt the harder steel saw blade. Countersink the screws.

3. Attach the extension.

This particular extension attaches to the miter gauge with screws rather than bolts. There are two reasons for this. First, it's fairly easy to adjust the position of the extension on your miter gauge — you just drill new pilot holes when you want to move it. Why not cut a long slot to make it even easier to adjust, you ask? That brings up the second reason: Many times, you can make more accurate cuts if you cut the extension as well as the workpiece — the workpiece is better supported against the rotation of the saw blade. Investing time in machining a jig you're just going to cut up makes no sense.

To attach the extension, use your miter gauge as a template to mark the location of the pilot holes. With the gauge in a table saw slot, place the extension against the face. Position the extension where you need it, then stick an awl or a pencil through the holes in the gauge and mark the wood. Drill ⅛″-diameter pilot holes at the marks. Secure the extension to the gauge with roundhead screws and washers. (See Figure 1.)

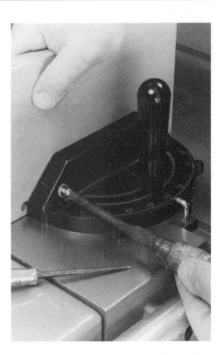

1/Attach the V-jig extension with roundhead wood screws and flat washers. Different makes of miter gauges may require different sizes of screws. If the extension mounting holes are very large, use fender washers instead of flat washers.

Self-Cleaning Radial Arm Saw Backstop

Keeping the backstop clean is a major nuisance when you use a radial arm saw. Sawdust collects at the fence, preventing you from butting your workpiece against the fence. Without the workpiece flat against the fence, any cut you make will be inaccurate. So you must brush the sawdust away after every cut.

The backstop shown is *self-cleaning*. One-eighth-inch-thick spacers create a narrow slot between the backstop and the back edge of the table. This groove is not wide enough to interfere with the normal operation of the saw, but it is wide enough to allow the sawdust to fall through. The table surface remains cleaner, and it's easier to make accurate cuts.

An adjustable stop makes it easy to cut duplicate parts. This small, wooden clamp attaches anywhere along the backstop. Turn the thumbscrew to fasten it in place.

Materials List

FINISHED DIMENSIONS

PARTS

A.	Backstop	¾″ x 2½″ x (variable)
B.	Spacers	⅛″ x (variable) x 1″
C.	Stop sides (2)	¾″ x 1⅞″ x 2″
D.	Stop spacer	¾″ x ⅞″ x 2″

HARDWARE

¼″ T-nut
¼″ x 1¼″ Thumbscrew

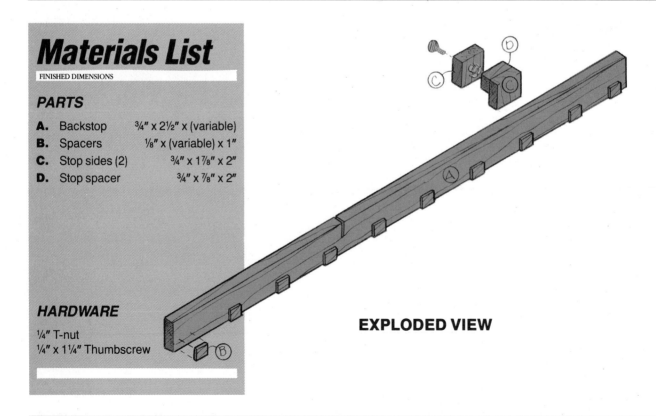

EXPLODED VIEW

1 Cut the parts. Measure the width (side to side) of your saw table to determine the length of the backstop. Also measure the thickness of the table.

This determines the height of the spacers — they should be ¼" *less* than the table thickness. When you have determined all the dimensions, cut the parts.

2 Assemble the backstop. Evenly distribute the spacers along the length of the backstop. (The spacing isn't critical. However, there should be no more than 3" between any two spacers.) Mark their positions, then glue them in place so the bottom edges of the spacers and the backstop are flush.

TRY THIS! Backstops get chewed up quickly by saw blades. While you're set up to make one, why not build two or three so you have some extras on hand?

3 Assemble the stop. In one side of the stop, drill a counterbore and a hole for the T-nut and thumbscrew. Insert the T-nut into the counterbore. (This may require a few sharp blows of a hammer.) Glue the parts of the stop together with the T-nut to the inside, as shown in the *Stop Detail/Side View.* Sand the glue joints clean and flush, then install the thumbscrew in the T-nut.

Use the stop like a small clamp. Position it on the fence to establish the length of pieces you need to cut in multiples. Tighten the thumbscrew to secure the stop. Lay a board against the fence with one end against the stop. Cut off the part you need. Slide the board along the fence until the end meets the stop, then cut another piece. Repeat until you have all the parts you need.

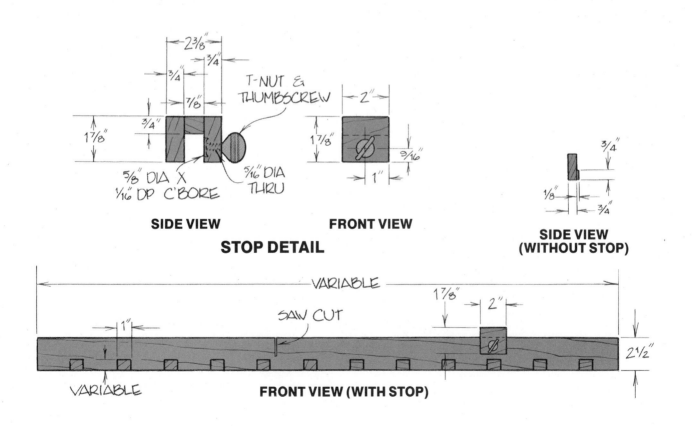

Tips for Using the Self-Cleaning Radial Arm Saw Backstop

Although this backstop truly is self-cleaning, it can use some help. To keep the dust on your saw table to a minimum, fit your radial arm saw with a dust collector such as the one shown in the Safety Tools chapter.

Keep a bench brush nearby to clear away large chips — these won't fall into the gap. Always ensure that your work is flat against the backstop *before* you cut it.

Tapering Jig

Many woodworking projects require you to make long, angled saw cuts — projects with tapered legs, posts, seats, braces, and other angled parts. Often, you must duplicate these angled cuts. For example, when making a chair seat, you must taper both sides. When a project has tapered braces, it probably has two or more of them. When building a table with tapered legs, you must cut all four sides of four table legs — sixteen cuts in all.

A tapering jig guides angled cuts precisely (and repeatedly) on a table

saw or radial arm saw. Set it to the angle needed — the jig shown is adjustable between 0° and 20°. It

holds each workpiece at the same angle to the blade as you push it along the rip fence or backstop.

Materials List

FINISHED DIMENSIONS

PARTS

A. Arms (2)   ¾" x 2" x 24"
B. Blocks (2)   ½" x 2" x 2"
C. Stop   ¾" x ¾" x 2"
D. Handle   1" dia. x 5½"

HARDWARE

2" Strap hinge and mounting screws
Curved lid support
#14 x 1" Panhead screws (2)
³⁄₁₆" Flat washers (4)

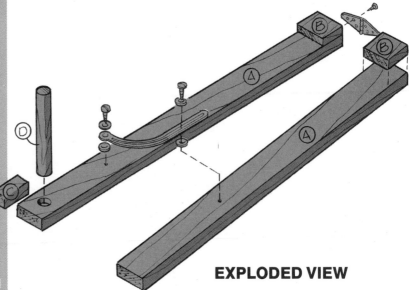

EXPLODED VIEW

1

Gather and cut the parts. Purchase a *curved* lid support. (The curve is important! A straight support will not work; it will extend over the side of the jig and hit the rip fence.) Remove the brackets from the support. On most, the brackets come off when you loosen a few screws, but you may have to drill out a rivet. (See Figure 1.)

The jig shown is 24″ long — long enough to cut most table legs. Decide whether this is the right length for you. Changing the length also changes the angle capacity. A longer jig has *less* capacity. For example, a 30″ jig adjusts up to only 15°. A shorter jig can be set to a wider range of angles. Consider making two jigs — one long, one short — so you can select the best one for the job. When you determine the length (or lengths) you want, cut the parts.

1/If necessary, drill out the rivet to remove a bracket from a curved lid support. Before drilling, mash the rivet with a hammer to keep it from turning.

2

Assemble the wooden parts. Glue a wooden block to one end of each arm. Drill a 1″-diameter, ½″-deep hole in one arm, as shown in the *Top View.* Glue the handle in this hole. Glue the stop to the edge of the handle arm, left of the handle (as you would hold it when using the jig). The back end of the stop and the arm should be flush.

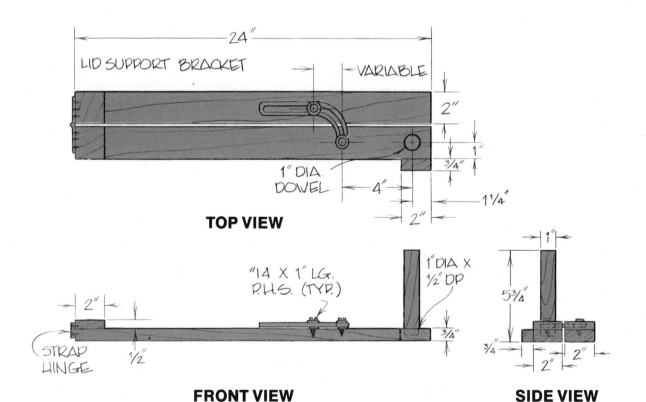

TOP VIEW

LID SUPPORT BRACKET — VARIABLE — 24″ — 2″ — 1″ DIA. DOWEL — 4″ — 1″ — ¾″ — 1¼″ — 2″

FRONT VIEW

STRAP HINGE — 2″ — ½″ — #14 X 1″ LG. P.H.S. (TYP.) — 1″ DIA X ½″ DP — ¾″

SIDE VIEW

1″ — 5¾″ — ¾″ — 2″ — 2″

3 *Assemble the metal parts.*

Sand all glue joints clean and flush. Clamp the arm together, and attach the strap hinge to the block ends. Remove the clamps.

Attach the curved lid support to the handle arm with a panhead screw and washers. Turn the screw until it's snug, but not tight. The support must be able to pivot easily on the screw.

Choose a location for the second screw — the screw that fits in the support slot — on the other arm, 1"-2" closer to the hinge than the first screw. Put the point of an awl through the support slot and hold it. Have a helper move the left (handle) arm back and forth while you observe the action of the lid support. It never should extend over the right edge of the jig. If it does, move the screw location closer to the hinge. If it doesn't, move it in the opposite direction. (See Figure 2.)

Experiment until you find the point where the second screw is as far as possible from the hinge, but the lid sup-

2/The location of the right (slot) screw will change with the make of the lid support. Using an awl, experiment to find the best place for the screw.

port never extends over the right side of the jig. Drill a pilot hole, and install the screw and washers. As before, turn the screw until it's snug, but not tight. The lid support should slide easily between the washers.

Tips for Using the Tapering Jig

There are two different types of information you can use to set the tapering jig. You can set it to a particular *angle* (degrees) or you can set it to a *slope* (inches over inches). Project plans show either the angle or the slope, but rarely both. The angle is the easiest to find — it's shown by a "°" mark. The slope usually must be calculated from dimensions listed on the *Side View* or *Front View*.

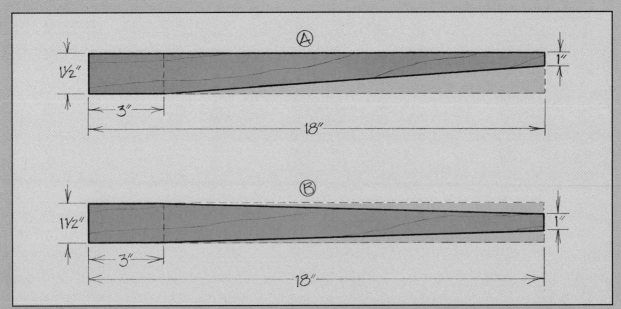

In drawing (a), an 18"-long leg tapers on one side, from 1½" wide at the top to 1" wide at the bottom. The taper starts 3" below the top of the leg. To determine the slope, subtract the smaller width from the larger width, and place the difference over the length of the **taper** (not the length of the leg). Thus, the slope is ½" over 15".

If the part tapers on two **opposing** sides, you must figure the slope for **both sides**. Subtract the smaller width dimension from the larger, but divide the remainder by 2 and use the result as part of the slope. Thus the slope in drawing (b) is ¼" over 15".

Tips for Using the Tapering Jig—Continued

1 To set the tapering jig to an **angle,** first draw the angle on a large sheet of paper.

2 Place the tapering jig on the angle you have drawn. Adjust the position of the arms so each one is parallel with one side of the angle. Tighten **both** screws.

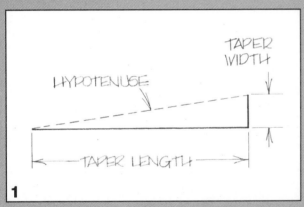

1 To set the jig to a **slope,** draw a right triangle on a large sheet of paper. Sketch the base (a) the same length as the taper, and the right side (b) the same width. Connect the base and the side to make the hypotenuse (c).

2 Place the tapering jig on the triangle you have drawn. Adjust the position of the arms so one is parallel with the base, and the other with the hypotenuse. Once again, tighten **both** screws.

3 After setting the taper, place the jig on your saw with the right arm against the fence. Place the workpiece against the left arm and butt the end against the stop. Adjust the position of the rip fence so the blade will start cutting at the proper place on the workpiece. Turn on the saw and push the jig forward, feeding the workpiece into the saw. (Saw guard removed for clarity.)

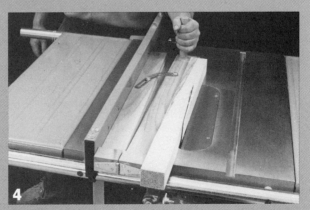

4 To make a second taper cut on the opposite side of the same workpiece, save the scrap from the first cut. Use this as a spacer to hold the workpiece at the proper angle in the jig for the second cut. (Saw guard removed for clarity.)

Resawing Fence

In the course of any woodworking project, you're likely to need several different thicknesses of wood. Planing wood to thickness is time-consuming and often wasteful, even if you have a thickness planer. Most home workshop planers are *finishing* tools. They remove only 1/16"-1/8" of stock in a single pass. If you have to reduce a lot of 4/4 stock to 1/4" thick on a planer, it will take you a long time — and you will be wasting most of the wood.

Resawing wood on the band saw saves lumber, if not time. Instead of getting a single 1/4"-thick piece from each 4/4 board, you can get two or three. Saw these boards to within 1/16" of the final thickness so you can finish them quickly on a planer, jointer, or belt sander.

To resaw wood accurately, you need a resawing fence to support

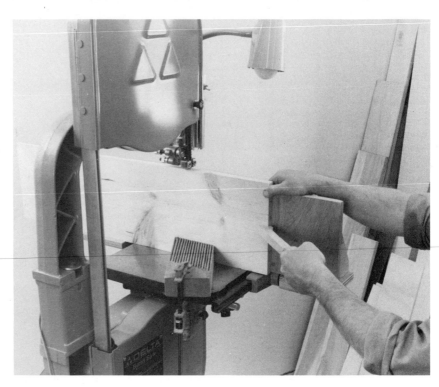

and guide the stock. The fence shown attaches to your existing band saw fence, if you have one, or it can be clamped directly to the work-

table. It provides an additional 6" of support on both the infeed and the outfeed sides of the table, making it easier to resaw long boards.

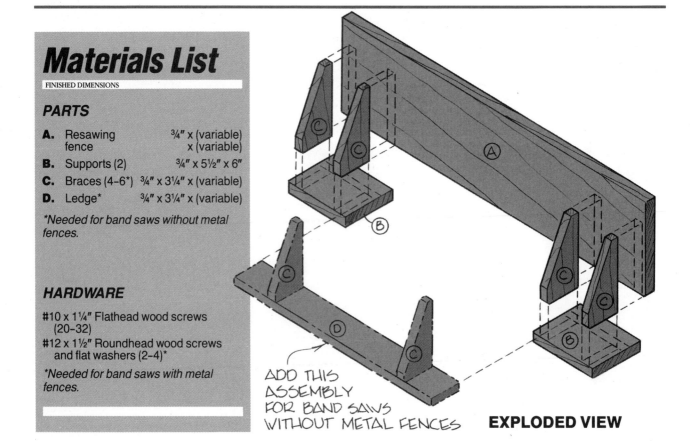

Materials List

FINISHED DIMENSIONS

PARTS

A. Resawing fence   3/4" x (variable) x (variable)

B. Supports (2)   3/4" x 5 1/2" x 6"

C. Braces (4-6*)   3/4" x 3 1/4" x (variable)

D. Ledge*   3/4" x 3 1/4" x (variable)

*Needed for band saws without metal fences.

HARDWARE

#10 x 1 1/4" Flathead wood screws (20-32)

#12 x 1 1/2" Roundhead wood screws and flat washers (2-4)*

*Needed for band saws with metal fences.

ADD THIS ASSEMBLY FOR BAND SAWS WITHOUT METAL FENCES

EXPLODED VIEW

1

Determine the dimensions. Measure the depth of your band saw worktable, from the infeed side to the outfeed side. Inspect the table for any protruding castings or attachments (guide rails, adjustment knobs, and so on) that might interfere with the resawing fence. Calculate the length of the fence — to the depth of the table add 12″ (total) for the infeed and outfeed supports, 1″ for clearance, and any allowances necessary for protrusions.

As mentioned, the fence either attaches to an existing fence or clamps directly to the worktable. If your band saw has a metal fence, check the location of the fence lock. You may have to shorten or modify the infeed support so you can reach the lock. (See Figure 1.)

If the band saw does *not* have a metal fence, you will have to add two braces and a ledge to the assembly. Use this ledge to clamp the fence to the worktable. (See Figure 2.)

Finally, decide how tall to make the resawing fence. It should be an inch or two shorter than the width of the stock you want to resaw. (If it's higher than the stock is wide, you won't be able to adjust the upper blade guides properly.) Some woodworkers make several different sizes of resawing fences so they can choose the best one for the job at hand.

Once you've determined what parts you need and their dimensions, cut them out. Taper the back edge of the braces, as shown in the *Side View.*

1/If your band saw has a metal fence, you may have to modify the infeed support so you can reach the lock. Allow at least 1″ clearance all around the lock handle.

2/If you don't have a metal fence, clamp the resawing fence to the worktable. Make the clamping ledge wide enough so your clamps will reach it.

2

Assemble the fence. Glue and screw the parts together, as shown in the *Front View* and *Side View.* Countersink the screws so the workpiece won't catch as you feed it along the fence.

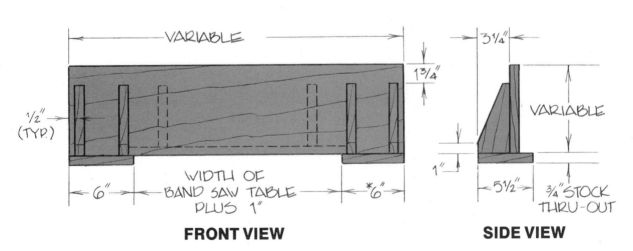

FRONT VIEW

VARIABLE

1¾″

½″ (TYP.)

6″

WIDTH OF BAND SAW TABLE PLUS 1″

*6″

SIDE VIEW

3¼″

VARIABLE

1″

5½″

¾″ STOCK THRU-OUT

* MAY HAVE TO BE REDUCED TO ACCOMMODATE FENCE LOCK

3 *Attach the fence to the band saw.*

If you have a band saw with a metal fence: All commercially made fences have holes so you can attach fixtures to them. The placement of these holes, however, varies with the make of the band saw. Use the metal fence as a template to locate matching holes on the wooden fence. Place the fences together on the band saw and mark the holes with a pencil or an awl. Drill pilot holes at these marks, then attach the resawing fence to the metal fence with roundhead wood screws and flat washers.

Ensure that the resawing fence is perpendicular to the worktable. If it isn't, adjust the metal fence. If the metal fence can't be adjusted, shim the wooden fence. Make shims out of thin strips of hardwood and glue them to the backside of the resawing fence, where it touches the metal fence. Pare the shims with a chisel until the resawing fence is absolutely perpendicular to the worktable.

If you don't have a metal fence: Clamp the resawing fence to the band saw and check that it's perpendicular to the worktable. If it isn't, you'll have to shim it. Glue the wooden shims to the underside of the ledge, where it touches the worktable. Shave the shims with a chisel or scraper until the resawing fence is absolutely perpendicular to the worktable.

Tips for Using the Resawing Fence

In addition to being perpendicular to the table, your resawing fence must also parallel the *drift* of the blade. Every band saw blade drifts slightly in a cut. The set of the teeth is never perfectly even, and the bite on one side of the blade will be a little greater than on the other. The blade will drift toward the side where the bite is greater.

If you set the fence parallel to the blade rather than the drift, the cut will be uneven. The blade will pull to one side, but the guides will prevent it from going too far. The blade will start to waver back and forth instead of cutting a straight line.

To find the drift of a blade, scribe a straight line on a long board. Turn on the saw, and start to rip the board along the line. Feed it slowly, feeling how the blade pulls. After cutting for a foot or so, you should be able to feed the board without swinging it back and forth to keep the blade tracking the line. *Without moving the board,* turn off the saw. Scribe a line on the saw table parallel to the edge of the board. This is the drift line.

Install the resawing fence parallel to this line. Be sure to position it so the board you produce will be 1/16"-1/8" thicker than the finished, planed stock should be.

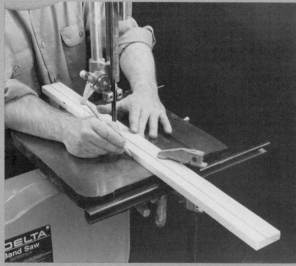

When you are able to rip your test board accurately without swinging it from side to side, hold the board in its position and turn off the saw. Using the board as a guide, scribe a pencil line on the saw table. This is the drift line. It probably will be a few degrees off parallel from the blade.

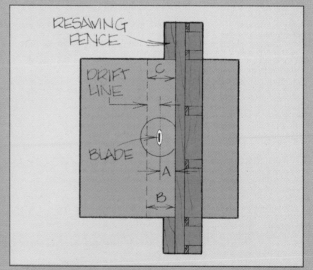

When you install the resawing fence, first measure the distance between the blade and the fence (a). This should be 1/16"-1/8" thicker than the final thickness of the stock you want to cut. Then measure the distance between the fence and the drift line at the infeed side (b) and the outfeed side (c) of the worktable. When these two measurements are the same, the fence is parallel to the line.

Tips for Using the Resawing Fence—Continued

Note: If you clamp your resawing fence directly to the worktable, simply shift the position of the fence to adjust it parallel to the drift line. If you attach it to a metal fence, you'll have to adjust the alignment of the metal fence. Consult the band saw owner's manual for instructions.

Here are a few more tips for resawing:

- Make sure the blade guides and the table are adjusted and aligned properly. Problems caused by misalignment magnify when resawing.
- Use the widest blade your saw will handle with as few teeth per inch as you can find. Narrow blades bend and cup when resawing, and too many teeth

will cause the machine to bog down. (It won't be able to clear the sawdust from the cut fast enough.)

- If the blade cups in the cut, adjust the blade tension *slightly* higher than the recommended setting. If it still cups, feed the wood more slowly.
- Use a fingerboard to keep the stock firmly against the resawing fence as you feed it. Position it slightly ahead of the blade, toward the infeed side of the table.
- Keep a pushstick or two within easy reach so you can finish the cut safely.

Fretwork Table

When making intricate cuts in small or thin workpieces, use a hand-held coping saw, fretsaw, or jeweler's saw. An electric-powered scroll saw is too cumbersome to cut small pieces, especially if the stock is thin. It's unsafe too — your fingers are too close to the blade. You can do these jobs better by hand.

Use a fretwork table to support the stock as you cut. This is a board with a slot and a hole cut in it to accommodate the blade. Clamp it to your workbench so the slot overhangs the edge.

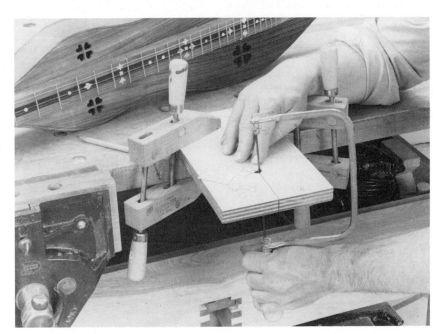

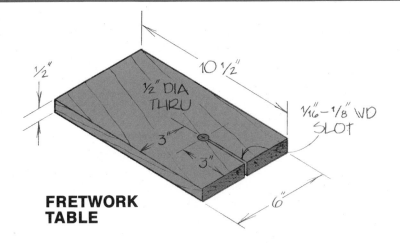

FRETWORK TABLE

½"

10 ½"

½" DIA THRU

1/16"–1/8" WD SLOT

3"

3"

6"

Materials List

FINISHED DIMENSIONS

PARTS

A. Fretwork table   ¾" x 6" x 10½"

1 Cut the table.   Make the table to fit the work you have to do. The table shown is for general work. Make yours smaller or larger, or make several sizes so you can choose the table that best suits the job. When you have decided, cut the table from hardwood.

2 Make the saw slot.   Mark the slot on the stock. (If you're making a larger or smaller table than what's shown, extend or shorten the slot proportionately.) Drill a ½″-diameter hole through the table at the *interior* end of the slot. Then cut the slot, starting at the exterior end and making a narrow kerf with a band saw or saber saw.

3 Attach the table to a workbench.   To use the table, clamp it to your workbench so the interior end of the slot is 1″-2″ from the bench's edge. Most of the fretsaw table should rest on the bench, not hang over the side. This will stabilize the work surface.

Tips for Using the Fretwork Table

Always mount the blades in the frame of your coping saw, fretsaw, or jeweler's saw so the teeth are pointing *down* as you cut. This will help hold the workpiece on the table. Pull up a chair or a stool to get comfortable, and make slow, steady cuts. Fretwork requires time and patience.

To cut extremely thin or fragile stock (such as veneer), sandwich it between two pieces of poster board or ⅛″-thick hardwood. Tape the sandwich together, and saw through all three layers. The poster board or hardwood will keep the thinner, more fragile stock from tearing or chipping.

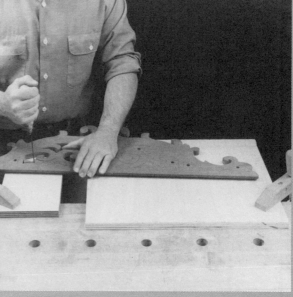

If you are sawing a long workpiece, clamp an extra board or two to the workbench (on one or both sides of the fretwork table) to provide additional support. These boards must be the same thickness as the fretwork table.

Drilling Tools

- Drill Press Table
- V-Jigs
- Drill Press Stop
- Drill Press Lathe Jig

Although it's a common tool in a woodworking shop, the drill press is a metalworking tool. Because of this, woodworkers can't perform all the necessary drilling tasks on the unadorned tool. To get full use out of your drill press, you must outfit it with several shopmade fixtures.

The *drill press table* is the most important of these. It expands the work surface, changes the tilt direction, and provides a backstop for your work. The *V-jigs* steady cylinders and disks while you drill them. The *drill press stop* is used in dozens of different setups. It will automatically locate holes in duplicate workpieces, evenly space holes along a board, stop a mortise at a predetermined point, and so on. Finally, the *drill press lathe jig* converts the drill press into a miniature lathe for turning gallery spindles, cabinet door pulls, doll furniture parts, and other small items. ✹

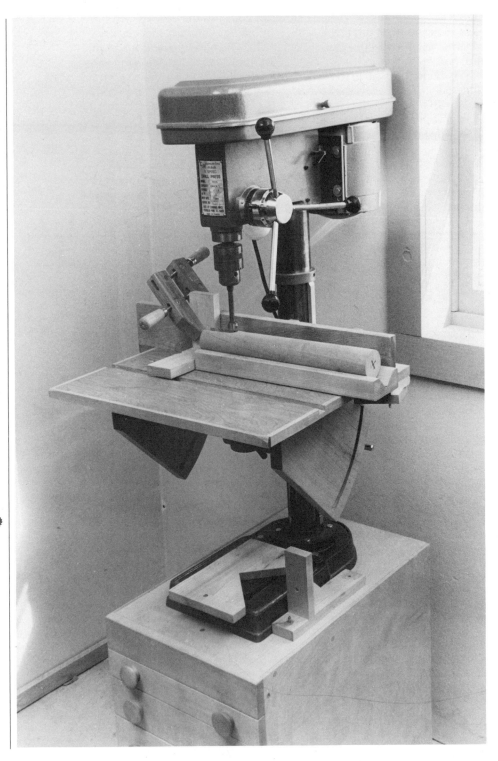

Drill Press Table

S tand-alone presses, whether they are bench tools or floor models, are engineered for *metalworking*. Only a few multipurpose tools, such as the Shopsmith or Total Shop, incorporate true woodworking drill presses.

The difference is all in the table. The standard drill press has a small table with mounting slots for a variety of vises and metal machining tools. The table tilts left and right, which is adequate when working with small metal parts.

Woodworking usually involves larger parts. The small table does not provide adequate support. The left/right tilt is confining: You can't drill an angled hole in the middle of a long part because the support column is in the way. The vise-mounting slots are unnecessary; what you need is a fence or a back-stop to hold and position the work.

The table fixture shown converts a standard drill press into a useful woodworking tool. Attached to the drill press, it quadruples the table size. The work surface tilts front-to-back, from 0° to 45°. A fence attaches anywhere on the table. A slot for a standard-size miter gauge lets you use this accessory to guide and position workpieces.

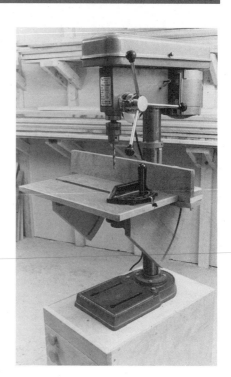

Materials List

FINISHED DIMENSIONS

PARTS

Table

A.	Table	¾″ x 16¼″ x 20½″
B.	Base	¾″ x 12″ x 14″
C.	Trunnions (2)	¾″ x 10⅛″ x 12″
D.	Braces (2)	¾″ x 1½″ x 12″

Fence

E.	Fence	¾″ x 3½″ x 24½″
F.	Fence base	¾″ x 2″ x 24½″
G.	Fence braces (4)	¾″ x 2″ x 2¾″
H.	Spacers (2)	¾″ x 1¾″ x 2¾″
J.	Clamps (2)	¾″ x 2¾″ x 3¼″

HARDWARE

#10 x 1¼″ Flathead wood screws (24–30)

⅜″ x 2″ Carriage bolts, flat washers, and wing nuts (2)

⅜″ x 3″ Carriage bolts, flat washers, and wing nuts (2)

1½″ x 14″ Piano hinge and mounting screws

#14 x 1″ Panhead screws (4)

³⁄₁₆″ Fender washers (4)

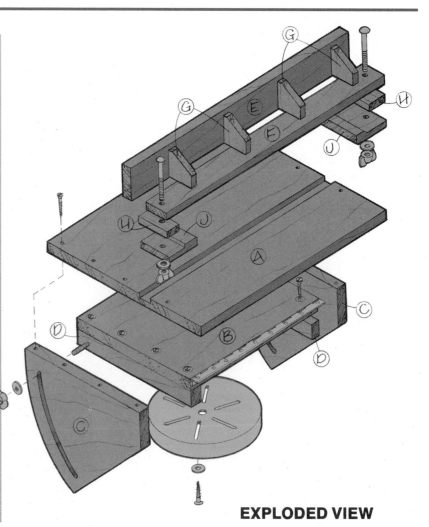

EXPLODED VIEW

1

Check the dimensions and cut the parts.
This drill press table fixture fits over a 12"-wide,
12"-deep metal drill press table, which is the size typical
of full-size drill presses (both bench and floor models).
Since many other sizes are manufactured, measure the
table on your drill press to be sure the fixture will fit. If
it won't, adjust the dimensions so it will. When you have
checked — and if necessary altered — all the dimensions,
cut the parts.

TRY THIS! For a durable table, purchase
a large, laminate-covered sink cut-out at a local
lumberyard or cabinet shop.

2

Cut the groove in the table. With a router
and a straight bit, cut a ¾"-wide, ⅜"-deep groove
near the front edge of the table. Test fit your table saw
miter gauge in this groove. The guide bar should rest
flush with the work surface, and the gauge should slide
along the groove easily with no play. If the groove is too
shallow or too narrow, remove a little more stock with
the router.

3

Cut the trunnions. Lay out the trunnions on
hardwood stock. Cut the outside shape with a band
saw or saber saw. Drill a ⁷⁄₁₆"-diameter hole at each end
of each curved slot. Remove the waste between the holes
with a saber saw, then file the edges of the slots smooth.

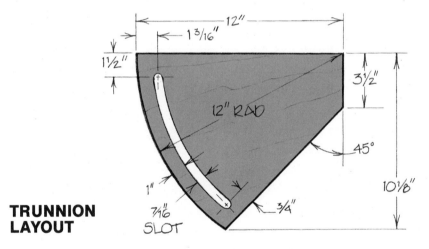

TRUNNION LAYOUT

4

Assemble the table. Glue the braces to the
base, and reinforce the joints with wood screws.
Countersink the screws.

Turn the table upside down on your workbench. Then
turn the base upside down and position it on the table.
Clamp the base to the table and install the piano hinge.
Remember, this hinge should be near the *front* of the
table, as shown in the *Top View* and *Side View.*

Attach the trunnions to the table with flathead
wood screws and glue. The ends of the trunnions must
be flush with the ends of the braces, and the screws must
be countersunk. When the glue dries, check the tilting
action of the table. Will it tilt through a full 45° without
the trunnions binding on the base assembly? If they do
bind, sand some stock off the edges of the base assembly.

Carefully brush away any sawdust between the base
and the table. Close the base flat against the table. Insert
a pencil or an awl in each slot and mark the location of
the ⅜"-diameter carriage bolt hole on each brace. Swing
the base clear of the trunnions and drill the holes. Swing

the base back again and insert the carriage bolt in the holes. The heads must be on the *inside.*

Once again, check the tilting action of the table. Will it tilt fully without binding? If the bolts bind, file or sand a little stock from the inside of the slots. When the table tilts properly, install flat washers and wing nuts on the bolts and tighten them.

5 **Cut the braces.**   Taper the back edge of each fence brace, as shown in the *Side View.* Use your table saw and a miter gauge extension to make the cuts. (See Figure 1.)

1/To cut duplicate tapers in the fence braces, use a long miter gauge and stop block, similar to those shown in the Sawing chapter.

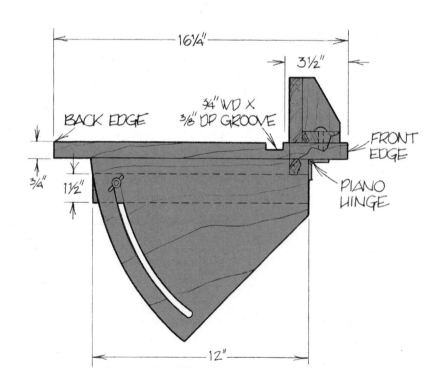

SIDE VIEW

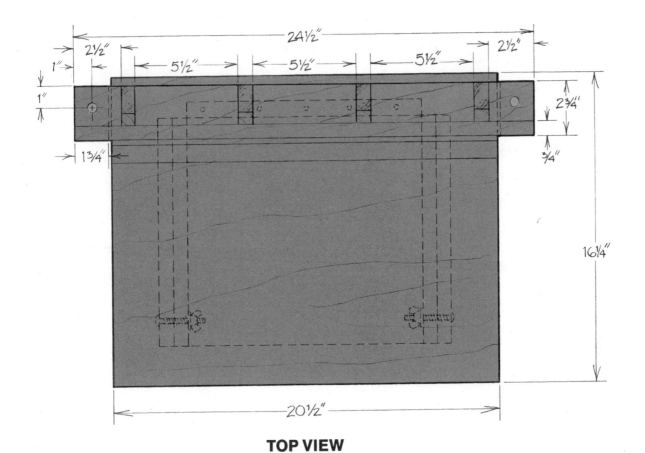

TOP VIEW

FRONT VIEW

6 Assemble the fence.

Glue and screw the fence braces to the base, then attach the fence. Countersink the screws.

With the assembly on a flat surface, check that the fence's face is perpendicular to the surface. If it isn't, plane the fence on a jointer. (See Figure 2.) Make sure the screws are far enough below the surface of the wood that they won't damage the jointer knives.

Glue the spacers to the fence assembly, even with the ends of the base. After the glue dries, sand the joints clean and flush. Drill a ⅜″-diameter bolt hole through each clamp block and each end of the fence. Using a band saw, cut a ⅛″ step in the top of each clamp block, as shown in the *Fence Assembly Detail*. Insert carriage bolts through the fence and the clamps. Put washers and wing nuts on the ends of the bolts (but don't tighten them) to hold the clamps to the fence.

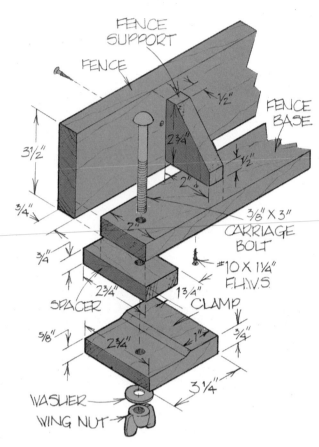

FENCE ASSEMBLY DETAIL

2/The face of the drill press fence must be perpendicular to the table. If it isn't, plane it on a jointer. Make sure the jointer fence is perpendicular to the jointer table. Hold the base flat against the fence as you pass the assembly over the knives.

7 Apply a finish.

Remove the hardware from the table and the fence, then lightly sand the wooden parts. Apply a penetrating oil finish, such as Danish oil or tung oil. When it dries, apply a heavy coat of paste wax.

This prevents glue from sticking to the wood, and keeps the table from becoming stained and dirty. It also helps work slide smoothly across the surface.

8 Attach the table to your drill press.

Reassemble the drill press table fixture. Remove the metal table from your drill press. This isn't as big a job as it sounds, since most tables are mounted with a single clamp or bolt.

Turn the wooden table upside down on a workbench. Invert the metal table, and center it on the wooden base. Drive #14 panhead screws with fender washers through the slots in the metal table into the wooden table. The fender washers will keep the screw heads from going through the slots. (See Figure 3.)

Reinstall the metal table — with the wooden table attached — on the drill press. Position the tables so

3/Attach the metal table to the wooden one with screws and fender washers. If the slots are too wide, or the tables shift even after being screwed together, drill ³⁄₁₆″-diameter holes through the metal table and drive screws through them.

they don't interfere with any controls — particularly the crank that raises and lowers the tables. Tighten the metal table in place.

9

Install the fence. Turn the clamps so the stepped (thick) ends face out. Place the fence on the table wherever you want it, turn the clamps around, and tighten the wing nuts to secure the fence.

Tips for Using the Drill Press Table

The drill press table has uses too numerous to list here. You'll discover some in this chapter, and still more as you begin to use the table. Here are a few general tips to get you started:

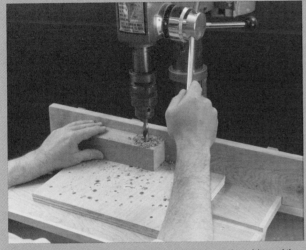

To protect the table, keep a scrap of wood between the table and the workpiece when drilling **through** stock. Use the drill press's depth gauge to prevent accidentally penetrating the scrap. In some cases, you may want to cover the table with a temporary work surface you can discard later.

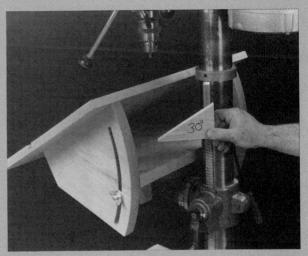

To adjust the table to a precise angle, cut a wedge from scrap wood to the angle you need. Use this as a feeler gauge between the table and the base. Set the gauge on the base, then rest the table on the gauge; the table will be tilted at the desired angle. You may want to keep wedges for commonly-used angles.

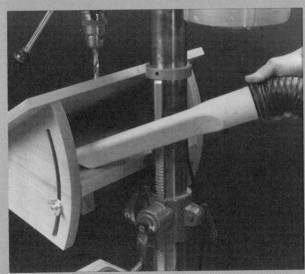

After drilling angled holes, and before returning the table to its horizontal position, clean out any sawdust or chips that may have fallen into the space between the table and the base. If sawdust collects here, the table won't rest perpendicular to the drill bit.

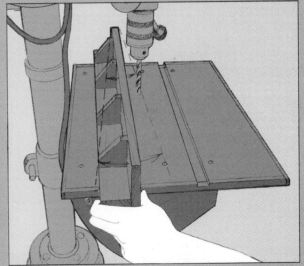

When adjusting the fence a precise distance from the bit, loosen both clamps to make coarse adjustments. Tighten one clamp, then move the opposite end of the fence forward and back to make **fine** adjustments. When the fence is properly placed, tighten the second clamp.

V-Jigs

Round and circular stock must be *cradled* to keep it steady when you're drilling it. A V-jig is a cradle. A *long V-jig* holds cylindrical stock, such as dowels and spindles. A *wide V-jig* holds circular or disk-shaped stock, such as wheels and bowls.

Although used principally with the drill press, these jigs will also hold workpieces for other power tools —table saw, radial arm saw, band saw, router, belt and disk sanders, to name a few. You can attach them to a miter gauge, guide

them along a rip fence or backstop, or clamp them to your workbench, or just use them freehand. In short, they can be used any time you need to cradle round or cylindrical stock and keep it rock-steady while you work on it.

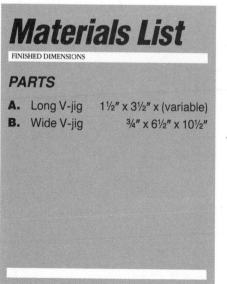

Materials List

FINISHED DIMENSIONS

PARTS

A. Long V-jig   1½" x 3½" x (variable)
B. Wide V-jig   ¾" x 6½" x 10½"

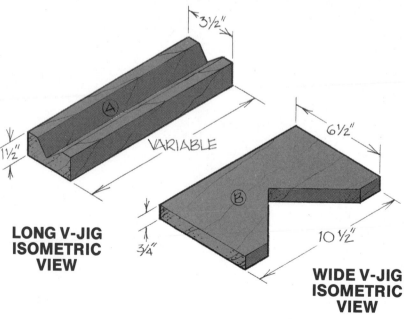

3½"

1½"

VARIABLE

LONG V-JIG ISOMETRIC VIEW

6½"

¾"

10½"

WIDE V-JIG ISOMETRIC VIEW

Making the Long V-Jig

1 ***Determine the length and cut the part.***
Consider the length and shape of the work that will be held in the V-jig, and cut the jig stock to the appropriate length. Cut several pieces; test cuts will reduce most to scrap. (As time goes on, you'll probably find you've accumulated a selection of V-jigs, each sized to a particular job you've done. That's the way it is with jigs.)

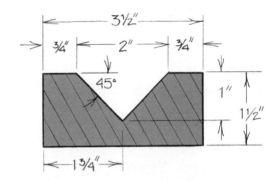

LONG V-JIG SECTION

2 ***Cut the V-groove.*** Tilt your table saw blade to 45° away from the fence. Adjust the saw height and the position of the rip fence so the saw teeth are 1″ above the table and 1¾″ from the fence. (See Figure 1.) Cut a scrap, turn it end for end, and cut it again. *Be very careful!* You must remove the saw guard to make these cuts. Use pushsticks and pushshoes to guide the stock and keep your fingers out of danger. Inspect the results — the cuts should form a 2″-wide, 1″-deep V-groove. If they don't, readjust the blade or the fence, and cut another scrap.

When the blade and fence are correctly positioned, cut the V-jig stock.

1/Position the blade and the fence so the saw teeth are 1″ above the table and 1¾″ from the fence. Then cut a scrap to check the setup. Don't be surprised if you need to reposition the blade or the fence. With the blade at an angle, it's difficult to measure the position of the teeth precisely.

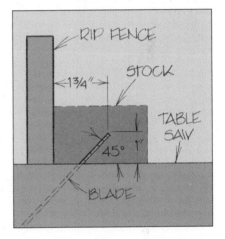

Making the Wide V-Jig

1 ***Cut the part.*** The wide V-jig shown will handle most disk-shaped wooden parts, up to 12″ in diameter. If the woodworking that you do involves larger disks, make a larger jig. Consider making two jigs — one for small parts, the other for large. When you are sure of the dimensions, cut the stock.

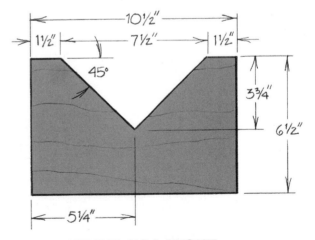

WIDE V-JIG LAYOUT

2 **Cut a V-shaped notch.** Lay out the notch on the stock, as shown in the *Wide V-Jig Layout*. If you're making a larger jig, increase the size of the notch proportionately. Cut the notch with a band saw or a saber saw.

Tips for Using the V-Jigs

To ensure the accuracy of your work when you use these jigs, use the fence or miter gauge to guide the jigs, or secure them to the fence or the table with hand screws and C-clamps.

Occasionally, you must secure stock in the jig. For the long V-jig, use flexible metal mending strap. (You can find it in the plumbing section of most hardware stores.) Bend the ends of each strap. Wrap the strap over the workpiece, insert a roundhead screw through each end, and drive the screws into the top of the V-jig. As you turn the screws clockwise, the strap will tighten over the stock. If it doesn't tighten enough, shorten the strap. Keep the strap from marring the workpiece with strips of leather.

Use this same method to secure workpieces in the wide V-jig. Wrap the strap around the edge of the workpiece and drive the screws on opposite sides of the notch.

Drill Press Stop

Simple devices can have enormous capabilities. That's the case with the drill press stop. It's just an L-shaped bracket — two pieces of wood screwed together. But it has dozens of uses on the drill press, alone or in combination with other fixtures such as the V-jigs. For example, when clamped to either the fence or the worktable, it will help you:

- Space holes evenly along a piece.
- Space holes evenly around the edge of a circular piece.
- Locate holes in duplicate workpieces.
- Position work precisely on the table when drilling compound angles.
- Stop mortises at a predetermined length.

These are just a few of the possibilities. As you begin to use this tool, others will occur to you.

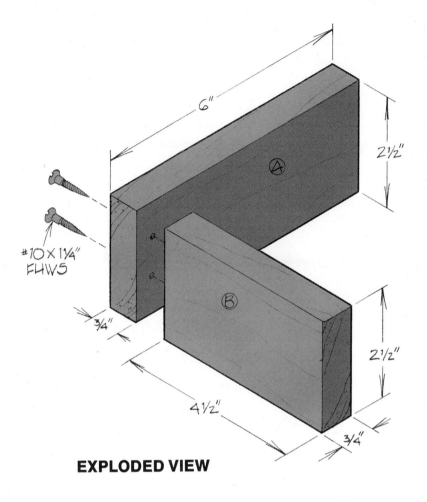

6"

2½"

#10 X 1¼"
FHWS

¾"

4½"

2½"

¾"

EXPLODED VIEW

Materials List

FINISHED DIMENSIONS

PARTS

A.	Long arm	¾" x 2½" x 6"
B.	Short arm	¾" x 2½" x 4½"

HARDWARE

#10 x 1½" Flathead wood screws (2)

1 **Cut the parts.** The stop shown will serve for most applications. Depending on a particular need, however, you may change the length of one or both arms. Decide what will serve you best, then cut the parts.

2 **Assemble the stop.** Glue the face of the long arm to the end of the short one. Reinforce the joint with screws, countersinking them.

3 **Check for squareness.** To get the most from this stop, the arms must be perpendicular to one another. Check this with a try square. If the assembly is out of square, remake the stop. When you're satisfied that it's square, sand the joints clean and flush.

TRY THIS! Double-check the alignment of your saw blade before you rip and cut the parts. This will ensure that the adjoining surfaces are square.

Tips for Using the Drill Press Stop

*T*he uses for the stop are many. Here are a few:

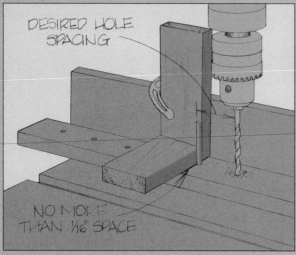

When drilling evenly spaced holes, clamp the stop to the fence above the workpiece. As shown, the distance from the stop to the bit must equal the desired, on-center spacing of the holes. Drill a hole, put a peg in it, and slide the workpiece toward the stop. When the peg hits the stop, drill another hole. Pull the peg out of the first hole, put it in the second, and repeat until you have drilled all the holes you need. For the setup to work properly, the peg must fit snugly in the hole and the stop must be no more than 1/16" above the workpiece. (If the peg is loose, it will give, throwing off the spacing. If the stop is too high, the peg may tip slightly when it hits the stop, again throwing the spacing off.)

Use a setup similar to that shown at left to drill holes evenly spaced around a disk. Clamp the wide V-jig to the worktable to hold and guide the stock. Clamp the stop to the fence to one side of the bit. Depending on the spacing of the holes, notching the arm as shown provides a better stop.

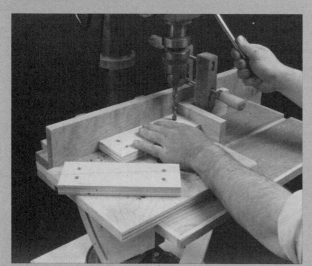

To expedite the production of duplicate parts, use the stop clamped to the fence to locate holes. Set the fence and the stop so the hole will be bored at the correct spot. Butt each workpiece in turn against the fence and the stop, then drill a hole. All the parts will be identical.

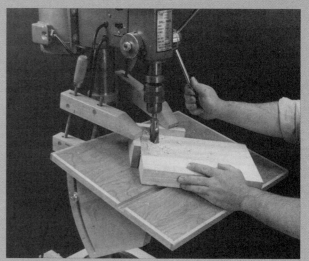

When drilling duplicate holes at a compound angle — such as round mortises to mount legs in a chair seat — use the stop as a V-jig to align the work at the proper angle. Clamp it to the high side of the table, the opening of the V facing down the table, the arms aligned to position the work at the proper angle. Butt the corner of the workpiece into the stop and clamp it to the table, too. Drill a hole, then repeat for other corners and other workpieces. All the holes will be at precisely the same compound angle.

Tips for Using the Drill Press Stop—Continued

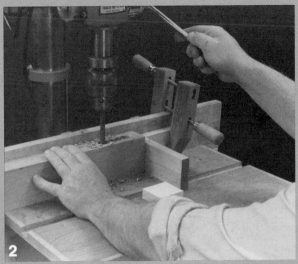

1. To make duplicate mortises, first cut a block of wood the same length as the mortise. Set up the fence and position the stop to halt the workpiece as you drill the far end of each mortise. To start the mortise, put the block of wood between the stop and the end of the workpiece. Drill the near end of the mortise.

2. Remove the block. Drill a series of holes to form the mortise, stopping when the workpiece hits the stop. Clean up the edges of the mortise with a chisel.

Drill Press Lathe Jig

Many project plans call for small, uncomplicated turnings — pegs, spindles, pulls, and so on. If you don't have a lathe, this can be frustrating. You'd like to build the project, but you don't want to invest in a major power tool to produce a few drawer pulls.

Using the jig shown with a drill press, you can turn small items, up to 2″ in diameter and 12″ long. You still will need a regular lathe to make larger pieces, like table legs or spindles for a staircase banister. And you must turn the wood vertically — a position that's not altogether comfortable for protracted work. Despite these drawbacks, the jig transforms your drill press into a workable turning machine.

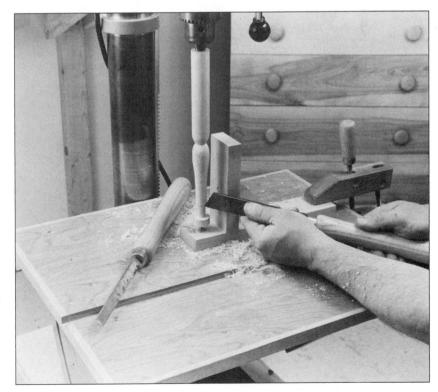

Materials List

FINISHED DIMENSIONS

PARTS

A.	Base	¾" x 2½" x 11½"
B.	Tool rest	¾" x 2½" x 7⅜"
C.	Brace	¾" x 4" x 4"

HARDWARE

¼"-dia. x 1½" Metal rod
#10 x 1½" Flathead wood screws (2)

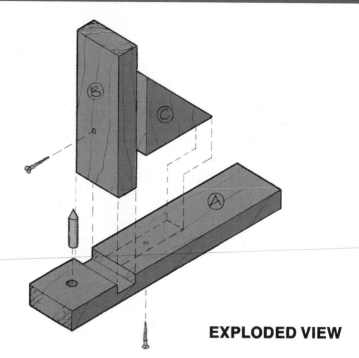

EXPLODED VIEW

---

1 **Cut the parts.** Select clear, hard wood to make this jig — the harder, the better. The tool rest takes quite a beating, and a soft wood won't last very long.

Choose the wood, then cut the parts. Cut the triangular brace on a band saw.

---

2 **Cut the dado and drill the hole.** Using a dado cutter or a table-mounted router, cut a ¾"-wide, ⅜"-deep dado across the base, 3" from one end. Drill a ¼"-diameter, ½"-deep hole, between the dado and the near end, as shown in the *Side View*.

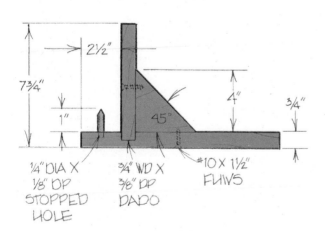

¼" DIA X ⅛" DP STOPPED HOLE

¾" WD X ⅜" DP DADO

#10 X 1½" FHWS

2½"

7¾"

1"

45°

4"

¾"

SIDE VIEW

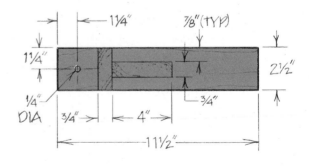

1¼"

⅞" (TYP)

1¼"

¼" DIA

¾"

4"

¾"

2½"

11½"

TOP VIEW

3 **Assemble the fixture.** Glue the tool rest in the dado, and the brace between the tool rest and the base. Reinforce the butt joints with flathead wood screws, countersinking the screws. Let the glue dry, then sand the joints clean.

4 **Make the tailstock.** Secure the metal rod in a hand-held electric drill like a drill bit. Hold the rod at an angle against a disk or belt sander, with *both* the drill and the sander running. The sander will quickly grind a smooth, uniform point on the rod. Let the rod cool, then insert it in the stopped hole in the base, point up.

Tips for Using the Drill Press Lathe Jig

When using the drill press lathe jig, follow this general procedure:

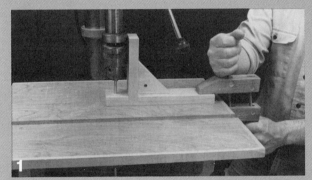

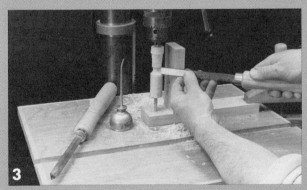

1. Secure the tailstock directly under the drill press chuck. To do this, clamp the tailstock loosely in the chuck and lower the chuck to the table. Clamp the base of the fixture to the table, release the chuck, and retract the drill.

2. Most turnings will be too large to fit into the drill chuck. Instead, drive a #12 screw into the stock, centered in the top end. Cut the head off the screw, and clamp the shank in the chuck. (When you've finished the turning, remove the screw with pliers.) Drill a ⅛″-diameter, ¼″-deep hole in the bottom end of the stock to fit over the point of the tailstock.

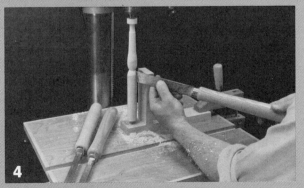

3. Run the drill press at a low speed. Turn the stock, using the tool rest to brace the chisels. Apply light pressure **only.** If you force the work, the tailstock hole may become enlarged; if it does, the stock will begin to wobble. Every fifteen minutes, apply a few drops of oil to the tailstock to keep the wood from wearing.

4. To turn stock longer than 6″, make the bottom of the turning first. Then flip the stock end for end on the jig, and turn the top portion.

Routing Tools

- Router Table
- Overhead Routing Fixture
- T-Square Routing Guide
- Mortising Jig
- Dovetail Spline Jig

The router is the oldest portable electric power tool, predating even the electric drill by several years. R. L. Carter, a patternmaker, fashioned the first crude router during World War I. He stripped a barber's electric clippers down to the motor and the worm gear. He ground the worm gear to make a cutter, then used the tool to finish some boiler patterns for the U.S. Navy. Woodworkers immediately recognized the capabilities of Carter's invention. In the ten years after the war, Carter sold over 100,000 routers.

Today, it's a common workshop tool. For many home craftsmen, the router is the primary tool for shaping wood and cutting joinery. The jigs and fixtures shown expand and simplify these applications.

The *router table* turns your router into a shaper. It also makes it easier and safer to cut joinery in small and medium-sized workpieces. The *overhead routing fixture* lets you feed work under a stationary router so you can rout round and odd-shaped pieces. The *T-square routing guide* simplifies cutting dadoes, grooves, and rabbets. Use the *mortising jig* to guide the router when making mortises and slots in long, narrow pieces, such as table legs or door stiles. With the *dovetail spline jig,* you can strengthen the corners of boxes and cases with decorative dovetail splines or keys. ●

Router Table

While the router is a versatile tool, a router table will more than double what you can do with it. Furthermore, it will improve the ease, accuracy, and safety of many common routing operations.

A router table holds the router upside down and provides a work surface so you can feed wood *over* a bit. If the bit is unpiloted, a fence guides the work. This gives you more control; it's usually easier to feed the workpiece than the router. A router turns at 20,000-25,000 rpm. This generates a great deal of *angular momentum* — the same force that keeps a bicycle upright or a top from tipping over. Because of this momentum, it takes muscle and

concentration to control the direction of the router. Since the workpiece doesn't spin, it requires less effort to control the wood as you pass it over the router.

A table also makes it possible to safely rout small pieces — parts that you couldn't clamp to your workbench because the clamps would block the router. It makes it easier to rout narrow boards (such as picture frames), since you don't have to move the clamps constantly. Finally, it makes your routing more accurate. It's easier to hold the work against a table and a fence; you can see what you're cutting. When you hold the router against the work, the router often blocks your view.

Commercial router tables are on the market, but there are advantages to making your own. Most of the manufactured tables are small, and the cheaper ones are often flimsy. None of the manufactured tables have a switched outlet. The miter gauges that came with even the best manufactured router tables are small and made of plastic.

You can make a large, sturdy table to better support the work. You can install wiring to turn the router on and off easily at the front of the table. You can cut a slot for your table saw miter gauge; most table saws have heavy-duty metal gauges.

In short, you can make a better table.

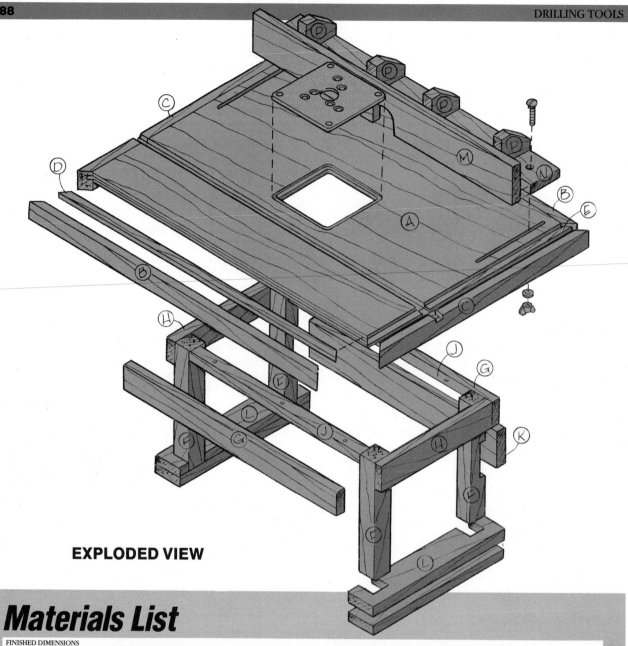

EXPLODED VIEW

Materials List

FINISHED DIMENSIONS

PARTS

Table

A.	Table	¾″ x 20″ x 29″
B.	Front/back trim (2)	¾″ x 1½″ x 30½″
C.	Side trim (2)	¾″ x 1½″ x 21½″
D.	Front/back splines (2)	¼″ x ¾″ x 29¾″
E.	Side splines (2)	¼″ x ¾″ x 20¾″
F.	Legs (4)	1½″ x 1½″ x 10¼″
G.	Front/back aprons (2)	¾″ x 2″ x 23½″
H.	Side aprons (2)	¾″ x 2″ x 13½″
J.	Ledgers (2)	¾″ x ¾″ x 19″
K.	Brace	¾″ x 3″ x 22″
L.	Feet (4)	¾″ x 2½″ x 15″

Fence

M.	Fence	¾″ x 3½″ x 30½″
N.	Fence base	¾″ x 3″ x 30½″
P.	Fence braces (4)	¾″ x 2¾″ x 3″

HARDWARE

Router mounting plate and mounting screws

¼″ x 2″ Carriage bolts, flat washers, and wing nuts (2)

#10 x 1¼″ Flathead wood screws (24–30)

#10 x 1¼″ Roundhead wood screws (6–8)

#10 x ¾″ Roundhead wood screws (2)

Combination switch/outlet

Metal switch box and outlet plate

Cable/box connector

14/3 Electrical appliance cord (10′)

Grounded plug

1 **Cut the parts.** As shown, the router table will hold a router that is up to 11″ tall with a 6″-diameter base. Most light-to-medium-duty portable routers are within these dimensions. Routers, however, come in all shapes and sizes. Measure yours *before* you start this project, and, if necessary, change the dimensions shown. Then cut the parts.

TRY THIS! For a durable table, buy a large, laminate-covered sink cut-out at a local lumberyard or cabinet shop.

2 **Prepare a mounting plate.** Purchase a router mounting plate from a mail-order woodworking supplier, or make your own from 3/16″-thick aluminum or high-impact polycarbonate plastic. (Look in the yellow pages under "Aluminum" or "Plastic Products.") Check that your router will fit the mounting plate shown, then cut the material and drill the holes as shown in the *Mounting Plate Layout.*

Remove the base from your router and center it on the mounting plate. Using the base as a template, mark *both* the router and the guide bushing mounting holes on the plate. (See Figure 1.) Keep in mind that you want to mount the router so the height adjusting mechanism is easily accessible from the front of the table — position the holes accordingly. Drill and countersink the holes to fit the screws that came with the router and the guides. File the plate to remove any burrs.

Note: It's not essential that you center the router precisely on the mounting plate. When you mark the hole locations, you can eyeball the position of the base.

However, you must carefully mark and drill the router and guide bushing mounting holes *at the same time.* The guide (when you use it) must be centered over the router.

*1/Using the router base as a template, mark the router and guide bushing mounting holes on the base. You need **both** sets of holes. Some router table operations require a guide.*

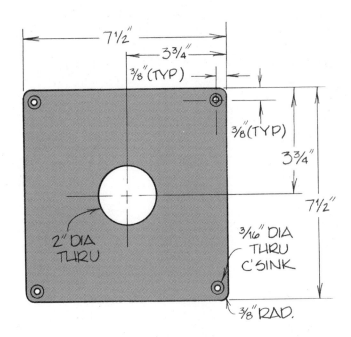

MOUNTING PLATE LAYOUT

3

Cut the router opening and slots in the table. Lay out the opening and the slots on the table as shown in the *Top View*. Drill a ⅜"-diameter hole at each corner of the opening layout, then cut between the holes with a saber saw to remove the waste. Using a router and a ¾" straight bit, cut a ¾"-wide, ³⁄₁₆"-deep rabbet around the perimeter of the opening to hold the mounting plate. (See Figure 2.)

Drill a ⁵⁄₁₆"-diameter hole through the table at each end of the fence slots. With a router and a ¼" straight bit, cut ¼"-wide slots between each set of holes. Clamp a straightedge to the table to guide the router. To widen each slot to ⁵⁄₁₆", move the straightedge ¹⁄₁₆" and rout the slot again. (See Figure 3.)

2/When you machine the rabbet for the mounting plate, clamp a straightedge to the table to guide the router. Cut the rabbet along one side of the opening, move the straightedge, and cut the next side. Continue until you have rabbeted the entire perimeter of the opening.

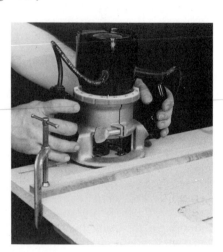

3/Rout the slots in several passes, cutting just ⅛"–¼" deeper with each pass. If you're using particle board or a laminate-covered material for the table, cut just ¹⁄₁₆"–⅛" deeper on each pass.

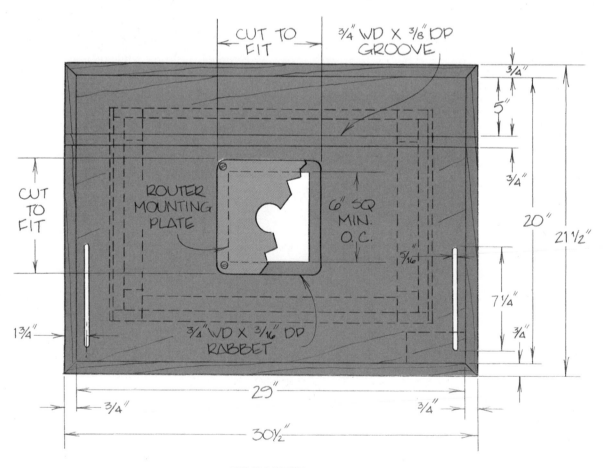

CUT TO FIT

¾" WD X ⅜" DP GROOVE

¾"

5"

¾"

20"

21½"

ROUTER MOUNTING PLATE

CUT TO FIT

6" SQ MIN. O.C.

⁵⁄₁₆"

7¼"

¾"

1¾"

¾" WD X ³⁄₁₆" DP RABBET

29"

¾"

¾"

30½"

TOP VIEW

4 ***Attach the trim to the table.*** Using a
slotting cutter and your router, cut ¼"-wide,
⅜"-deep grooves around the edge of the table. Some
slotting cutters only cut ½"-deep grooves. If you have
one of these, make the splines 1" wide. (See Figure 4.)
Without changing the setup, cut matching grooves in the
trim. Miter the ends of the trim and the splines to fit the
perimeter of the table. Test fit the parts to be sure all the
mitered ends meet properly, then glue the splines and
the trim to the table. Let the glue dry, then scrape the
joints clean and flush.

Note: If you've used a laminated sink cut-out for the
table, don't sand the top edge of the trim — you may
scratch the laminate. Use a scraper instead.

4/A slotting cutter
has 2-4 cutting teeth
spaced evenly around
a plate, which is
mounted on a piloted
arbor. The diameter
of the plate deter-
mines the depth of
the slot and the thick-
ness of the teeth
determines the width.
The router's depth
adjustment controls
the location of the slot
in the edge of the
workpiece.

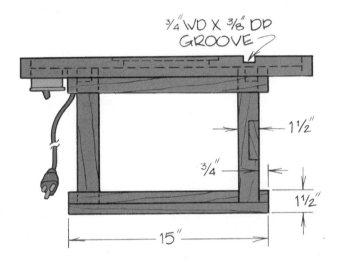

SIDE VIEW

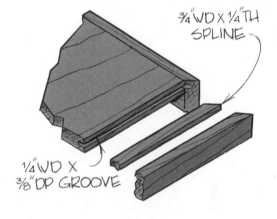

EDGE-TO-TOP DETAIL

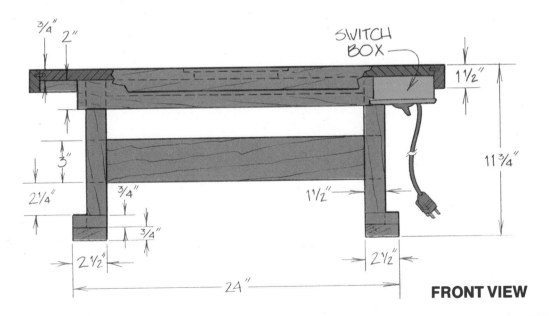

FRONT VIEW

5 **Cut the groove in the table.** With a router and a straight bit, cut a ¾"-wide, ⅜"-deep groove near the front edge of the table. Test fit your table saw miter gauge in this groove. The guide bar should rest flush with the work surface, and the gauge should slide along the groove easily with no play. If the groove is too narrow or too shallow, remove a little more stock with the router.

6 **Cut notches in the back legs and top feet.** Lay out the notches on the back legs (as shown in the *Front View* and the *Side View*), and on the top feet (as shown in the *Top Foot Layout*). Cut the notches with a band saw or saber saw. Test-fit the brace and the legs in the appropriate notches.

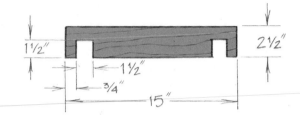

TOP FOOT LAYOUT

7 **Assemble the base.** Glue the top feet to the bottom feet and set them aside until the glue dries. Glue and screw the aprons together, as shown in the *Base/Top View*. Glue the legs and the ledgers to the apron assembly, then the feet to the legs. Last, glue the brace in the notches in the back legs.

Reinforce all glue joints with flathead wood screws, counterboring and countersinking the screws. Cover the screw heads with wooden plugs, then sand the plugs and the glue joints flush and clean. Round the hard edges and corners of the assembled base with sandpaper.

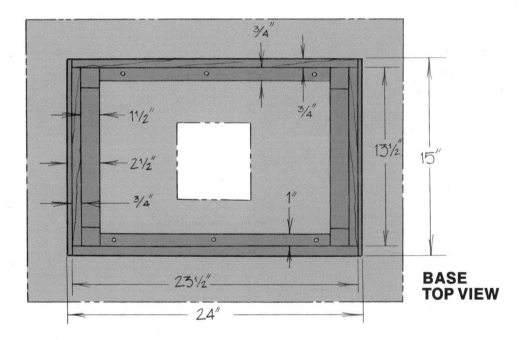

**BASE
TOP VIEW**

8 **Attach the base to the table.** Turn the table upside down on the workbench. Turn the base upside down and center it on the table. Clamp it in place, then drill pilot holes in the ledgers. Drive round-head wood screws through the ledgers into the table, joining the two assemblies. Remove the clamps.

9

Install a switch, plug, and power cord.
For safety and convenience, you should install
a switch under the table so you can quickly cut off the
power to the router. While the router table is upside
down on the workbench, attach a metal electrical box.
Place it near the front edge, toward either the left or
the right side (depending on whether you're left- or
right-handed).

Remove a knockout from the back side of the box,
install a box connector in the opening, and insert a
grounded appliance cord through the connector. Strip
the wires and attach the wires to a combination switch
and outlet. (See Figure 5.) The black wire attaches to
either of the brass screws, the white wire to the silver
screw, and the green (ground) wire to the green screw.

Install the switch/outlet in the electrical box, pulling
any excess cord out through the connector. Tighten the
connector's cable clamp, and install an outlet plate. Last,
attach a grounded plug to the cord.

*5/When you install
the switch/outlet, do
not remove the metal
tab (shown by the
arrow). With the tab in
place, the switch will
control the power to
the outlet.*

Warning: Before you plug the cord into a wall outlet,
check the electrical connections with a circuit tester.

10

Install the mounting plate. Turn the
router table over and set the mounting plate in
the rabbet around the router opening. The plate must be
flush with the table's surface. If it is too high, use a chisel
to shave the rabbet deeper; if too low, shim it up with

strips of paper, cardboard, or veneer. When the plate fits
properly, attach it to the table with flathead wood screws.
If necessary, file the heads of these screws level with the
plate's surface.

11

Make the fence parts. Using a miter gauge
extension and stop block, similar to those shown
in the Sawing chapter, cut the top back corners of the
fence braces. Drill a ¼″-diameter hole through the fence

base, near each end, as shown in the *Fence/Back View*
and *Fence/Top View*. With a saber saw, cut the notches in
the center of the fence and the fence base. These notches
will fit around the router bit.

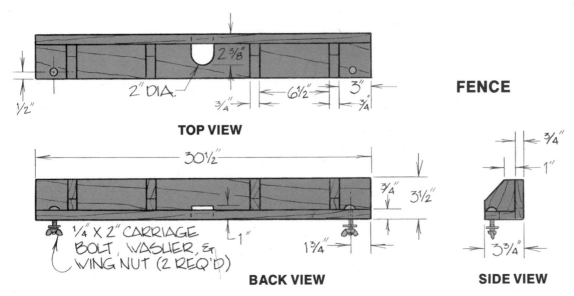

FENCE

TOP VIEW

BACK VIEW

SIDE VIEW

12 Assemble the fence.

Assemble the fence.   Glue the fence braces to the base, then to the fence. Reinforce the joints with flathead screws. Counterbore and countersink the screws, and cover the heads with wooden plugs. When the glue dries, sand the plugs and the joints flush and clean.

Set this assembly on a flat surface and check that the fence's face is perpendicular to the surface. If it isn't, plane the fence square on a jointer. (See Figure 6.) Make sure that the screws are far enough below the surface of the wood that the jointer knives won't hit them.

6/The fence must be perpendicular to the router table. If it isn't, plane it on a jointer. Make sure the jointer fence is perpendicular to the jointer table. Hold the base flat against the jointer fence as you pass the assembly over the knives.

13 Attach the fence to the table.

Attach the fence to the table.   Insert a carriage bolt through each ¼″-diameter hole in the fence base. Place the fence on the table so the bolts go through the slots. Secure the fence to the table with flat washers and wing nuts.

14 Apply a finish.

Apply a finish.   Remove the hardware from the table and the fence, then lightly sand the wooden parts. Apply a penetrating oil finish, such as Danish oil or tung oil. When the oil dries, apply a good coat of paste wax and reassemble the project. This finish prevents glue from sticking to the wood, and keeps the table from becoming stained and dirty. It also helps workpieces slide smoothly across the surface.

Tips for Using the Router Table

The router table has uses too numerous to list here. Use it to cut joinery, make moldings, even duplicate patterns. Here are a few general tips:

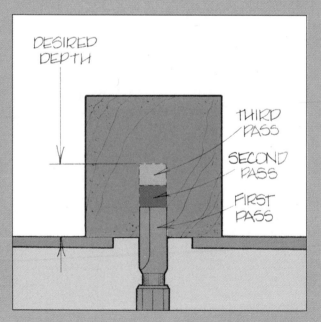

Never try to remove more than ⅛″–¼″ of stock from a board on a single pass. To make a deep cut, make several passes, raising the bit after each pass. To make uniform deep cuts in several pieces, make a shallow cut in each. Raise the bit, and make another pass with each workpiece. Continue until you have cut all the pieces to the same depth. Or: If your router is equipped with a stop, use it to stop each cut at the same depth.

Tips for Using the Router Table—Continued

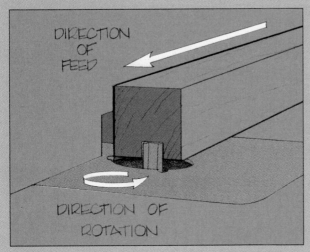

Always feed wood into a bit so the rotation helps to hold the wood against the fence. Since the bit rotates counterclockwise (as you look at the table from the top), feed a workpiece from right to left (as you stand at the front of the table).

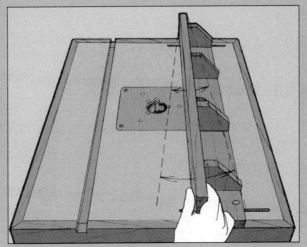

When adjusting the fence a precise distance from the bit, loosen both wing nuts to make **coarse** adjustments. Tighten one nut, then move the opposite end of the fence forward and back to make **fine** adjustments. When the fence is properly placed, tighten the second nut.

Overhead Routing Fixture

Mounting a router upside down in a table is a great boon, but there are times when you need the router to be right side up. By passing the workpiece *under* the router, you can cut mortises and grooves in round stock, make flutes in turned spindles, and rout odd-shaped boards. An overarm router holds the router in this position, but this is an expensive tool — too expensive to buy for occasional use.

An overhead routing fixture is the next best thing. It does almost everything an overarm router will do, and for a lot less money. The fixture clamps directly to your workbench and holds the router several inches above a work surface so the bit extends beneath the jig. Adjust the general height of the bit by loosening the wing nuts and raising or lowering the carriage. Make finer adjustments with the router's own height adjustment.

Materials List

FINISHED DIMENSIONS

PARTS

A. Carriage bottom   ¼" x 17" x 7¾"

B. Carriage
    front/back (2)   ¾" x 1½" x 15½"

C. Carriage sides (2)   ¾" x 1½" x 7¾"

D. Legs (2)   ¾" x 7¾" x 8"

E. Feet (2)   ¾" x 2¼" x 7¾"

HARDWARE

#10 x 1¼" Flathead wood screws (10)
#8 x ¾" Flathead wood screws (6)
⅜" x 2" Carriage bolts, flat washers, and
    wing nuts (4)
Mounting screws to fit router (3)

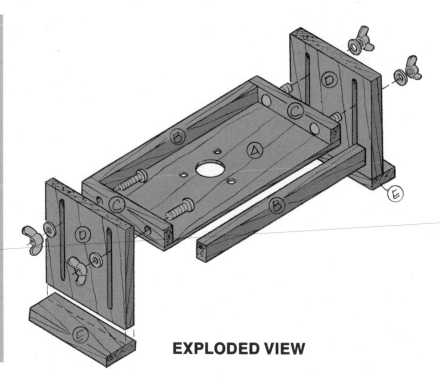

EXPLODED VIEW

1 **Cut the parts.** As shown, the overhead routing fixture will hold a router with a 6"-diameter base, which includes most light-to-medium-duty units. Routers, however, come in all shapes and sizes. Measure yours *before* you start this project.

Depending on the work you have to do, you may want the router held higher than the jig shown holds it. If so, you will have to lengthen the legs. If you lengthen them beyond 12", lengthen the feet 2"-3", too. Add braces between the feet and the legs to keep the fixture steady.

Consider these possibilities and, if necessary, make changes to the dimensions shown. Then cut the parts.

TRY THIS! Consider making the carriage bottom from clear, high-impact plastic. This will make it easier to see your work.

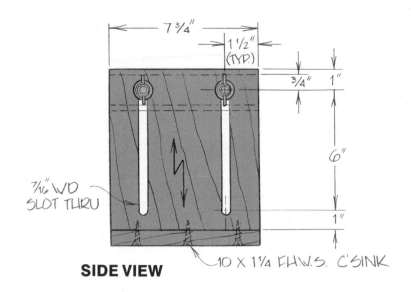

SIDE VIEW

2 Drill the carriage sides and bottom.

Drill ⅜″-diameter holes through the carriage sides, as shown in the *Side View*. With a hole saw or fly cutter, make a 2″-diameter hole in the center of the carriage bottom, as shown in the *Top View*.

Remove the base from your router and center it on the carriage bottom, over the 2″-diameter hole. Using the base as a template, mark the mounting screw holes on the workpiece. Drill and countersink the holes to fit the screws that hold the base to the router. **Note:** It's not essential that you center the router precisely on the carriage. When you mark the hole locations, you can eyeball the position of the base.

3 Cut the slots in the sides.

Lay out the slots on the legs, as shown in the *Side View*. Double-check your layout by placing a carriage side on top of each leg. The bolt holes must line up with the slots. If they don't, change the locations of the slots.

Drill a ⁷⁄₁₆″-diameter hole to mark each end of all four slots. Remove the waste between each set of holes with a saber saw, and file the edges of the slots smooth.

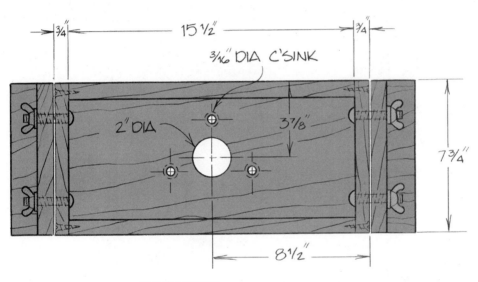

TOP VIEW

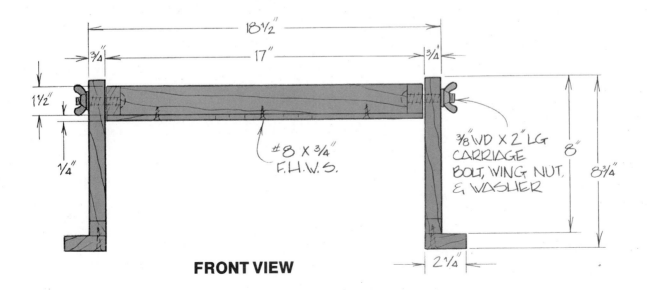

FRONT VIEW

4 **Assemble the jig.** Glue the carriage sides to the front and back. Reinforce the glue joints with flathead wood screws, countersinking the screws so they are slightly below the surface. Glue and screw the carriage bottom to this assembly. Let the glue dry, then sand the joints clean and flush.

Glue the feet to the legs, and reinforce the joints with screws. Once again, countersink the heads of the screws

slightly below the surface. When the glue dries, sand the joints.

Insert carriage bolts through the holes in the carriage sides. Fit the legs over the bolts, and check the sliding action. The carriage should slide up and down without binding. If it binds, file away a little stock from inside the slots. When the carriage slides smoothly, secure the legs with flat washers and wing nuts.

Tips on Using the Overhead Routing Fixture

Every power tool and accessory presents certain hazards, and this fixture is no exception. In addition to the safety procedures that you follow when using a router, *never place your hands under the carriage when the router is plugged into an outlet.* Always

clamp the fixture to the workbench before turning on the router.

Here are some additional thoughts on using this fixture:

When you adjust the height, measure from the carriage to the table at **all four corners** to be sure the router is level. Move the carriage to make **coarse** height adjustments, then use the router's height adjustment mechanism to make **fine** corrections.

To guide long cuts, such as mortises and flutes, clamp a straightedge to the table. This will guide the workpiece (or the jig in which it rests) under the router. This straightedge should be no taller than the work, so you can lower the carriage as close to the work as necessary.

To cut blind mortises, grooves, and dadoes, first drill a hole at each end of the cut. Position the piece under the router and — with the router **off** — lower the bit into one of the holes. Hold the workpiece firmly on the table and against the straightedge, then turn the router on. Rout from hole to hole and turn it off. If necessary, make several passes to cut to the desired depth. Remember to turn the tool off each time you change the height of the bit.

Tips on Using the Overhead Routing Fixture—Continued

You can **pin-rout** small parts with this fixture. Pin-routing is a technique for reproducing small patterns and parts. Drill a ⅜"-diameter stopped hole in your workbench, and insert a metal rod long enough to protrude ¼"-⅜" above the bench. Chuck a ⅜" straight bit in the router, and lower the bit until it almost touches the top of the rod. Position the fixture so the bit is directly over the rod, and clamp the feet to the workbench.

Place the assembly on the workbench with the pattern facing down. Adjust the bit height so it will cut ⅛"-¼" into the blank. Rout the pattern in the blank, letting the pin (metal rod) guide the work. Make several passes, lowering the bit ⅛"-¼" with each pass, until the pattern reaches the desired depth — or you cut through the blank. Loosen the screws to remove the work from the pattern.

Cut the pattern with a scroll saw or jigsaw. Glue it to a base. Screw the piece you want to machine to the other side of the base. Be careful to position the screws where the router bit won't hit them.

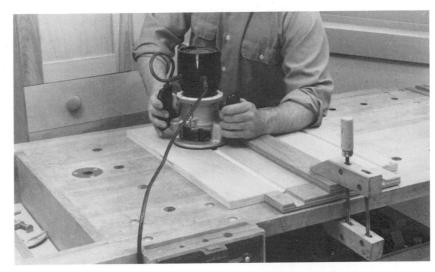

T-Square Routing Guide

Routers are great tools for making dadoes, grooves, and rabbets, particularly in plywood and large stock. You may make these cuts quicker with a saw-mounted dado cutter, but plywood splinters easily and large workpieces are difficult to maneuver. A router leaves a smooth cut, even in plywood, and it is easier to handle than a hefty board. The only drawback is that a router requires a time-consuming setup: You must measure and mark the joint, measure and mark the location for the guide, then clamp the guide in place.

This T-square routing jig simplifies the chore. You simply mark the *location* of the cut (you don't have to mark the entire length), line up the appropriate groove in the T-square with the mark, and clamp the jig to the workpiece. There's a lot less measuring and marking.

Materials List

FINISHED DIMENSIONS

PARTS

A. Guide   ¾" 3" x 30"
B. Crossbar   ¾" x 3" x 14"

HARDWARE

#10 x 1¼" Flathead wood screws (3)

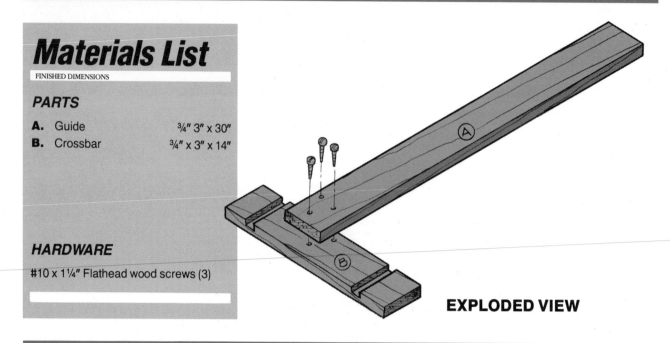

EXPLODED VIEW

1 **Cut the parts.** There are two edges to the T-square routing jig, and you can use each to cut a different-sized joint. On the jig shown, one edge guides the router when cutting with a ¾" bit, and the other with a ½" bit. You may also want to make a jig for ⅜"- and ¼"-wide cuts. Decide how many jigs you need, then cut the parts from clear hardwood.

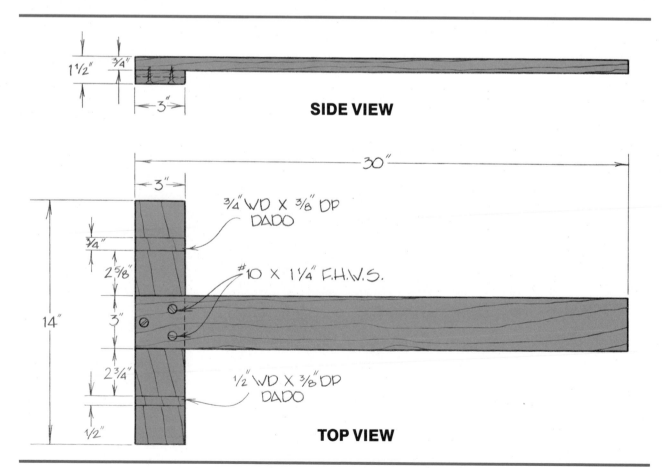

SIDE VIEW

1½"   ¾"   ←—3"—→

30"

3"

¾" WD X ⅜" DP DADO

¾"
2⅝"
3"
2¾"
½"

14"

#10 X 1¼" F.H.W.S.

½" WD X ⅜" DP DADO

TOP VIEW

2 Joint the parts.
The guide and the crossbar must be perfectly straight. To make them so, joint *both* edges of the guide, and one edge (the edge that will rest against the workpiece) of the crossbar.

3 Assemble the jig.
Glue the crossbar to the guide. As you clamp the parts together, check that they are square to one another. Check again after you tighten the clamps. *This is crucial!* The parts must be perfectly perpendicular, or the jig will be useless.

After the glue dries, sand the joint clean. Check the alignment of the guide and crossbar again, just to be sure. Drive three screws to reinforce the joint, arranged as shown in the *Top View.*

4 Rout the dadoes in the crossbar.
Set a large scrap across your workbench. Place the jig on the scrap, butting the crossbar against the edge. Clamp the jig to the scrap.

Fit a ¾″ straight bit in your router and select the edge of the jig you want to use for ¾″-wide joints. Keeping the base of the router firmly against the guide, rout a dado in the chosen side of the crossbar. Replace the ¾″ bit with a ½″ bit, and rout the other side. If you have made a second jig, repeat with ⅜″ and ¼″ bits.

Tips for Using the T-Square Routing Guide

The use of this jig is straightforward: Butt the crossbar against the workpiece, line up the dado with your mark, clamp the jig, and rout the joint. There are a few tricks, however. To make accurate cuts, you must compensate for the limitations of your router.

When you remove the router base (when you install it in a router table, for example), then replace it, the base doesn't always return to the same position. There is play in the screw holes. Depending on the router, the base can shift up to ¹/₁₆″. Over time, each dado in the crossbar will become wider — as though the bit is shifting — making it useless for aligning the jig. Though you may line up the edge of the crossbar dado carefully with your mark, you will never know precisely where the cut will be.

To avoid this problem, paint alignment marks on the router and its base. Whenever the base must be removed from the router, you know you can return it to exactly the same position. When using the router in conjunction with a guide, position the alignment marks away from the guide, so they don't wear off.

*Plainly mark the router so you always replace the base in exactly the same position. Most routers have three base mounting screws. Paint a dot on **both** the base and the body between two of them. Each time you attach the base, align the dots. Start the screws in the holes, shift the base as far as it will go toward the dots, **then** tighten the screws.*

Tips for Using the T-Square Routing Guide—Continued

When you rout using a guide, always hold the router with the dots (indicated) facing away from the guide. That way, they won't rub off.

Mortising Jig

A router simplifies mortising operations. It will cut straighter, smoother slots in less time than an expensive mortising attachment for your drill press.

You can use several different jigs, including the router table and the overhead routing jig shown in this chapter, to help cut mortises. But the best one for the job is this mortising jig. It will help with all types of mortises — open, blind, stopped, and through. You can easily see what you're cutting and check your work as it progresses. The jig works with most rectangular workpieces, but it's especially designed for use with long, narrow pieces such as table legs and frame parts — just the kind you're most likely to mortise.

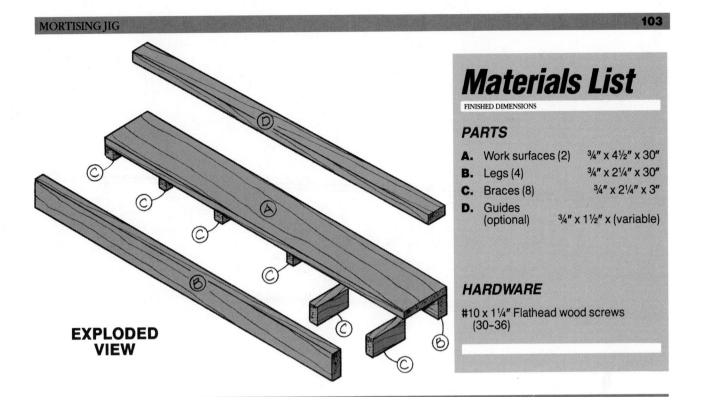

EXPLODED VIEW

Materials List

FINISHED DIMENSIONS

PARTS

A. Work surfaces (2)   ¾" x 4½" x 30"

B. Legs (4)   ¾" x 2¼" x 30"

C. Braces (8)   ¾" x 2¼" x 3"

D. Guides (optional)   ¾" x 1½" x (variable)

HARDWARE

#10 x 1¼" Flathead wood screws (30–36)

---

1 **Cut the parts.** This jig consists of two identical assemblies. (The workpiece is held between the two.) The drawings show only one assembly; be sure to cut the parts you need to make *two*.

---

2 **Assemble the parts.** To make each assembly, glue the braces between the legs, then glue the work surfaces to the legs. Reinforce the joints with flathead wood screws, countersinking each screw so the head is slightly below the surface. Let the glue dry, then sand the joints clean and flush.

Note: Do *not* attach the guides; these clamp to the work surfaces.

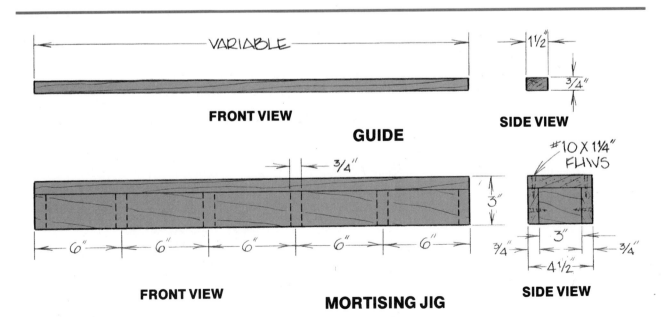

FRONT VIEW

SIDE VIEW

GUIDE

FRONT VIEW

SIDE VIEW

MORTISING JIG

Tips for Using the Mortising Jig

The jig is a worktable that *surrounds* the workpiece, providing stable bearing for the router, even if the workpiece is very narrow. When using the jig, follow this general procedure:

1

Clamp the workpiece between the halves of the jig. (Bar clamps work best; they provide even pressure along the length of the jig.) Both work surfaces and the upper face of the workpiece must be flush.

2

Clamp, nail, or screw the guides to the work surfaces. (The locations of the guides depend on the width and the location of the mortise that you want to cut.) If the mortise is blind, attach stops to restrict the router's range of movement. Make the stops from scraps, and mount them perpendicular to the guides.

3

Use a straight bit or a mortising bit to rout the mortise. Make several passes, cutting ⅛"–¼" deeper with each pass, to reach the desired depth. To make mortises deeper than ¾", use special 2"-long straight bits.

Dovetail Spline Jig

Mitered corners on boxes and cases have little strength unless you reinforce them. One way to do this — and add visual interest at the same time — is to install dovetail keys or splines across the miter joints. Cut the grooves for these splines with a router, a dovetail bit, and a dovetail spline jig.

The jig shown works with all sizes of projects. Small assemblies can be set in the jig, which is then passed over a table-mounted router. When the project is large, clamp the jig to it. Attach the guide to the jig's base and cut the grooves with a hand-held router.

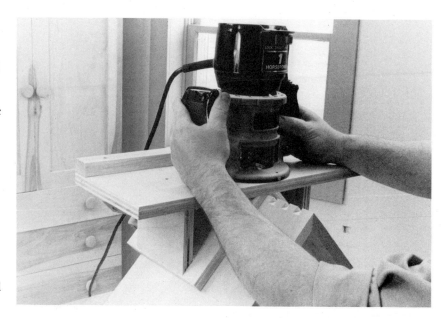

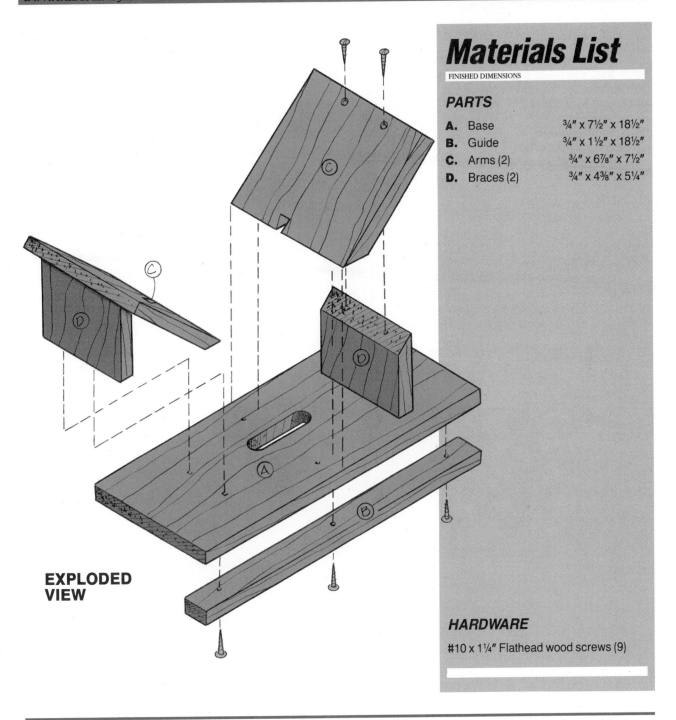

EXPLODED
VIEW

Materials List

FINISHED DIMENSIONS

PARTS

A. Base $3/4'' \times 7\frac{1}{2}'' \times 18\frac{1}{2}''$
B. Guide $3/4'' \times 1\frac{1}{2}'' \times 18\frac{1}{2}''$
C. Arms (2) $3/4'' \times 6\frac{7}{8}'' \times 7\frac{1}{2}''$
D. Braces (2) $3/4'' \times 4\frac{3}{8}'' \times 5\frac{1}{4}''$

HARDWARE

#10 x 1¼" Flathead wood screws (9)

---

1   ***Cut the parts.***   Select clear hardwood or cabinet-grade plywood to make the jig. Cut the parts to the sizes in the Materials List, and miter one end of each cradle and brace.

---

2   ***Cut the slot in the base.***   Mark the slot on the base, as shown in the *Base Layout*. Drill a 1"-diameter hole at each end of the slot, then remove the waste between the holes with a saber saw.

3

Assemble the jig. Assembling the jig can be tricky, because you can't clamp the mitered parts. With glue on them, they tend to shift and slide. To prevent this, glue and *nail* the braces to the arms. Place the nails where you will later install screws. Don't drive the heads of the nails into the stock. Let them protrude so you can remove them easily.

Glue and screw the arm assemblies to the base. Check the angle between the arms; they should be *precisely* perpendicular to each other. If they aren't, remove the nails from one of the arm assemblies. Shift the parts so the arms are perpendicular, then replace the nails. As the glue sets, pull the nails one by one and replace them with screws. Countersink all the screw heads slightly below the surface.

Screw (but *don't* glue) the guide to the base. Depending on the size of the workpiece you want to cut, you may want to remove the guide.

4

Cut dovetail grooves in the arms. Clamp the jig in a vise, base up. Chuck a dovetail bit in your router and adjust the height so the bit will extend ½″ *beyond* the jig's base when the router rests on the jig. Place the router on the jig so the bit is in the slot. Turn the router on and cut dovetail grooves through each arm.

Note: As you use the jig, try not to enlarge its dovetail groove. If you preserve the initial size, you can use it to "sight" where you will cut each groove on a project.

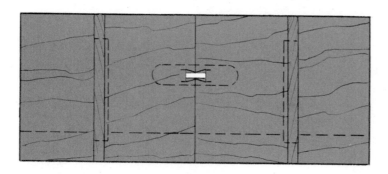

TOP VIEW

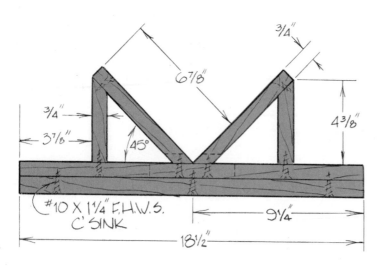

FRONT VIEW

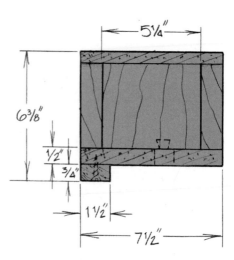

SIDE VIEW

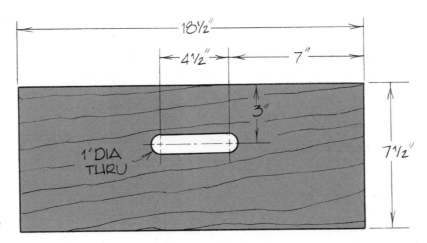

BASE LAYOUT

Tips for Using the Dovetail Spline Jig

When using the jig, follow this general procedure:

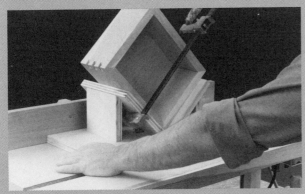

For a large project, clamp the jig to a corner and slide the router along the guide. For a smaller project, clamp the piece in the jig. Remove the guide and cut the grooves on a router table, using its fence as a guide.

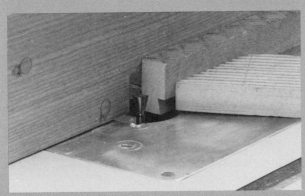

To make the dovetail splines, first cut a dovetail tenon along the edge of a board using a table-mounted router. Rip the tenon free of the board on a band saw, then cut it into 1" lengths.

Glue the splines in the dovetail grooves. Let the glue dry, then cut them off as close to the wood's surface as you can without scratching it. Sand the ends of the splines flush with the wood.

Joinery Tools

- **Tall Fence Extension**
- **Miter Jig**
- **Finger Jig**
- **Tenoning Jig**

After you have cut the parts for a woodworking project, you must join them together. There are endless ways to do this — butts, rabbets, dadoes, grooves, miters, mortises, tenons, finger, and dovetail joints, to name a few. A few jigs that attach to your saws, router, and jointer can greatly facilitate making all of these joints.

Each of the jigs will work with two or more power tools. The *tall fence extension* holds a wide board at the proper angle to a blade or cutter while you work the edge. It fits on the table saw, jointer, and router table. The *miter jig* cuts miters between 22½° and 45°. While a miter gauge will do the same thing, this jig is more accurate and requires less setup time. It works with either a table saw or a radial arm saw. The *finger jig* will cut fingers that interlock to form a finger joint, or knuckle joint. It's used on a table saw (with a dado cutter) or a table-mounted router. The *tenoning jig* holds long, narrow workpieces so you can make cuts in the ends. It straddles and slides along the rip fence of a table saw, or a guide board clamped to your router table.

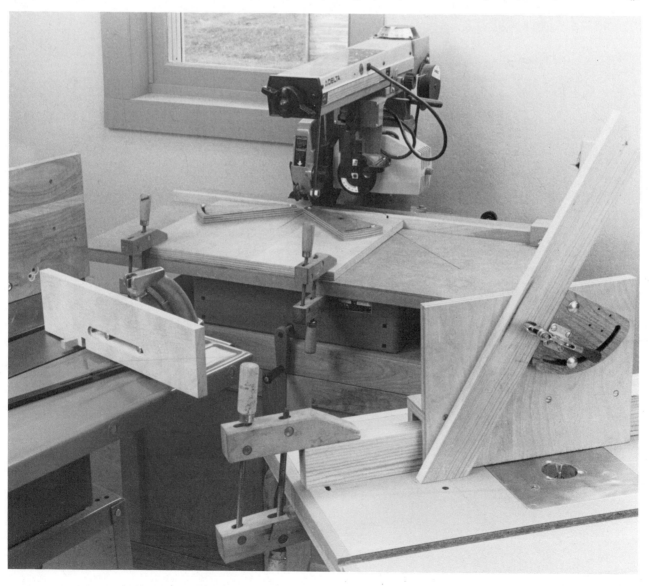

Tall Fence Extension

Fences on commercial power tools usually are less than 3″ high. These will not adequately support wide boards when you do edge work. If more than 6″ or 7″ wide, the board becomes unstable when standing on edge — even braced against the fence. The bottom edge tends to slide, away from the fence. The edge may be ruined before you finish the cut.

A tall fence extension solves this problem. A 10″-wide extension, attached to a power tool fence, safely supports 20″-wide boards when they're on edge. The extension is braced horizontally and vertically to remain flat and straight even when you apply heavy pressure — as long as the pressure isn't *too* heavy.

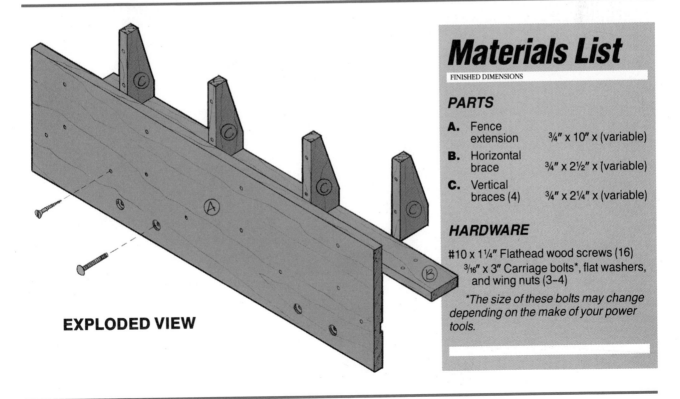

EXPLODED VIEW

Materials List

FINISHED DIMENSIONS

PARTS

A. Fence extension   ¾″ x 10″ x (variable)

B. Horizontal brace   ¾″ x 2½″ x (variable)

C. Vertical braces (4)   ¾″ x 2¼″ x (variable)

HARDWARE

#10 x 1¼″ Flathead wood screws (16)

³/₁₆″ x 3″ Carriage bolts*, flat washers, and wing nuts (3–4)

The size of these bolts may change depending on the make of your power tools.

1 ***Cut the parts.*** Measure the length and height of the fences on any of these tools you have — table saw, jointer, and router table. Make this extension to fit the longest *and* the tallest of the tools. You can adapt a large extension to fit a small fence, but it's difficult to do it the other way around. Determine the dimensions, then cut the parts.

2 ***Drill the bolt holes.*** All commercial saw and jointer fences have holes for mounting jigs, but the hole spacing varies from tool to tool. To mark the hole locations on the extension, use each fence as a template. Clamp the extension against the table saw rip fence, making sure the extension rests on the table surface, and the front edges of the fence and the extension are flush. Stick an awl or a pencil through the holes in the fence and mark them on the extension. Repeat for the jointer.

The router table fence probably has no holes. After you've drilled the holes in the extension for the first two tools, bore holes in the router fence.

Check the diameter of the holes in the saw and jointer fences. Most are 3/16″, but yours may be different. At each of the marks, drill a 5/8″-diameter, 1/4″-deep counterbore, then a smaller hole through the extension. The smaller hole should be the same diameter as the holes in the fences.

Now place the extension on the router table and hold it against the fence. Choose one set of the holes — saw or jointer — and mark them on the fence. Remove the fence from the table and drill a 3/16″-diameter hole at each mark.

Note: On some makes, it may be easier to attach the fence with screws.

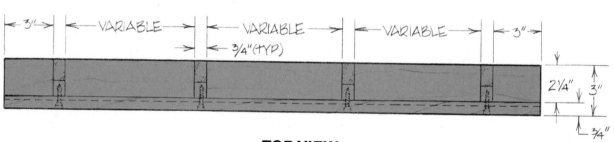

TOP VIEW

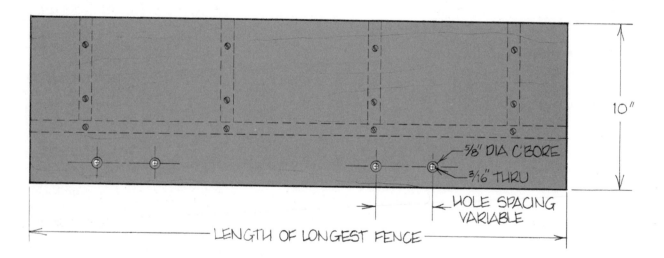

FRONT VIEW

3

Cut the braces. Taper each vertical brace, as shown in the *Side View.* Use your table saw and a tapering jig to make the cuts. (See Figure 1.)

1/To cut identical tapers in the vertical braces, use the tapering jig shown in the Sawing chapter.

4

Assemble the fence. Glue the vertical braces to the horizontal brace, then glue both parts to the extension. Reinforce the joints with flathead wood screws, countersinking them. When the glue dries, sand the joints flush and clean.

Tips for Using the Tall Fence Extension

When you use the extension, hold the wood against the extension firmly, but not so hard that it tilts. Apply most of the pressure as close to the horizontal brace as is practical.

In addition to doing edge work, you can also use the extension as a hold-down by clamping fingerboards to it.

#10 X 1¼"
FHWS

¾"

1"

¼"

VARIABLE

2"

¾"

2½"

HEIGHT OF TALLEST FENCE PLUS ¼"

¾" WD X
¼" DP DADO

SIDE VIEW

Miter Jig

Few joints demand more precision than the miter joint. Because the fit of any one miter depends on the accuracy of the others in the assembly, the smallest error will be compounded. For example, if you cut a 45° miter just ¼° too small or too large, the two boards joined by that miter will be ½° off square. With the next miter, the assembly will be 1° off, and so on. When you join the frame, the original ¼° error will have grown to 2°, enough to create a large gap in one of the joints.

You can achieve the necessary precision with the saw's miter gauge, but only with time and patience — and a lot of scrap wood for test cuts. Then you undo all your patient setup work when you return the gauge to 0° after making the miters.

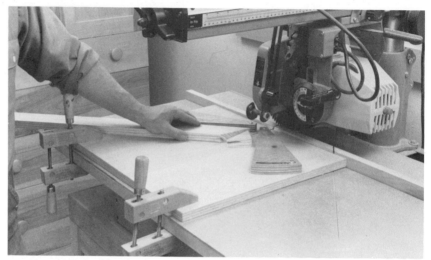

The miter jig shown ends that frustration. It's adjustable between 22½° and 45°, but once set, you can leave it at that setting. You can build it for a table saw or a radial arm saw, and set it to make both left- and right-facing miters. Whenever you want to cut a miter joint, set it on the saw.

Materials List

FINISHED DIMENSIONS

PARTS

A. Base   ¾" x (variable) x 20"
B. Pivots (2)   ¾" x 5⅞" x 10"
C. Guides* (2)   ⅜" x ¾" x (variable)

HARDWARE

#12 x 1¼" Roundhead wood screws
   and flat washers (2)
¼" x 1¼" Panhead screws and flat
   washers (2)
1" Brads* (10–12)

*Needed for table saw jig only.

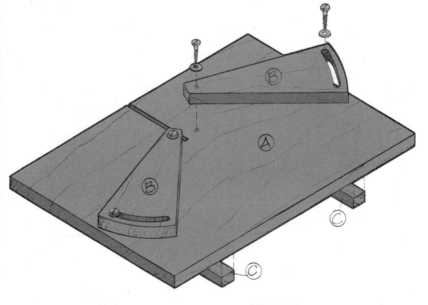

EXPLODED VIEW

1

Cut the parts.   Measure the saw table. On a table saw, measure from the front (infeed) edge of the table to the saw arbor. On a radial arm saw, measure from the front edge to the backstop. This measurement is the depth of the jig and the length of the guides (if needed). Cut the base and guides from cabinet-grade plywood.

2

Make the pivots.   Lay out the pivots on clear, hardwood stock or cabinet-grade plywood. Cut the outside shape with a band saw or a saber saw. Drill 5/16" holes — two in each pivot — delineating the ends of each curved slot. Cut the slots with a saber saw and file the edges smooth from cabinet-grade plywood.

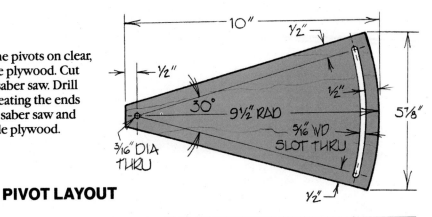

PIVOT LAYOUT

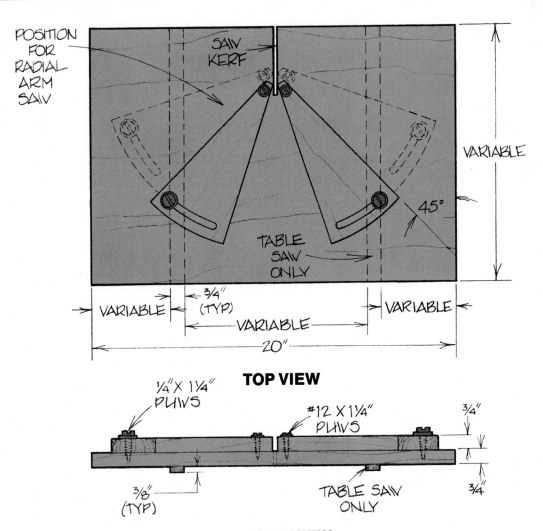

TOP VIEW

FRONT VIEW

3

Attach the guides to the base (table saw only). Place the guides in the miter gauge slots. They should be flush with the table surface and slide easily with no play. If they bind, remove a little stock with a sander. If they are too loose, remake them.

Lower the blade completely. Put the base on the table, centered over the guides. Mark the position of each guide on the front and back edge of the base. Remove the base and put a line of glue on each guide. Replace the base, lining up the marks with the guides, front and back.

Drive four brads through the base and into the ends of each guide to hold them in place. (Don't seat the brads; you will remove them later.) Remove the assembly from the table saw and wipe any glue off the tool.

Invert the base. Tack the guides to the base with brads, and set them. Remove the brads from the top side of the base. Let the glue dry, then lightly sand the guides clean.

4

Assemble the jig. Raise the table saw blade ¾"-1". Set the base on the table, guides in the slots. Turn on the saw, and slide the base into the blade, cutting a 3"-4" slot. On the radial arm saw, set the base against the backstop. Center the jig under the blade. Cut a 4"-5" kerf into the leading edge.

Remove the jig from the saw. Pick a point on the kerf, about 2" from the edge. Draw two lines extending from this point, one to the right, the other to the left, each 45° from the kerf. (See Figure 1.)

Align a pivot with each line. On the table saw, place the pivots on the infeed side of the lines. On the radial arm saw, place them on the side nearest the backstop. Position the narrow end so it almost meets the kerf. Fasten this end to the base with a roundhead wood screw and flat washer. Then drive a large panhead screw (with a flat washer) through each slot. (Don't place the screw all the way at the end of the slot. Allow room for adjustment.)

Turn all of the screws until they are snug but not tight. Check the action of the pivots — they should

1/Draw two lines on the base, extending out from the kerf at 45°. Align the pivots with these lines and fasten them to the base.

swing back and forth easily. If one binds on its panhead screw, remove it and file some stock from inside the slot.

5

Align the jig. When both pivots work smoothly, put the jig aside. Carefully check the alignment of the saw. On a table saw, the blade must be parallel with the miter gauge slots for the jig to work accurately. On the radial arm saw, the blade must track perpendicular to the backstop.

Set the jig on the saw. (If you're using a radial arm saw, line up the kerf with the blade.) With the saw turned off, move the jig (or the blade) so the blade is as deep in the kerf as it will go. Use a combination square to align the right and left pivot at 45° to the blade. (See Figure 2.) Tighten all the screws.

Cut a small frame using *just* the left pivot. Make sure all the sides are the same length, and put the mitered ends together. If the miters gap at the *inside, reduce* the angle. If they gap at the *outside, increase* it. Make a small adjustment and cut another frame. Continue this routine

*2/Make the initial alignment with a combination square. Make sure the gauge rests flat against the pivot **and** the blade — not against one of the saw teeth.*

until you have the left pivot properly set. Repeat the whole adjustment process for the right pivot.

Tips for Using the Miter Jig

Each time you use the gauge, check the alignment of the saw before you cut good stock. This is particularly important on the radial arm saw, which must be aligned often.

Hang the jig where you won't bump into it with a board or tool and knock it out of alignment. Don't lean it against a wall — you might accidentally kick it. Should you bump it, kick it, or drop it, test the alignment before using the jig again.

To duplicate frame parts with this miter jig, first make an L-shaped extension fence from a 1 x 2 and a 1 x 1, as shown in the photo. Screw this fence to one of the pivots, then clamp a stop block to the fence. Use the stop to automatically gauge the length of each frame part as you cut it.

Finger Jig

A finger joint uses evenly spaced, interlocking pins, or fingers, to join two boards. The fingers must be cut with precision on both boards or you won't be able to assemble the joint. The joint is a machine-made one that is not difficult to cut with a finger jig.

The jig shown spaces the notches for you with mechanical precision. Attach it to a miter gauge; you can adjust its position right and left. A small stop, the same width as the notches you plan to cut, extends from the face of the jig. By shifting the jig on the miter gauge, you adjust the distance between the stop and the cutter or bit. This, too, should be the same as the notches. After cutting each notch, shift the workpiece toward the stop, setting the newly cut notch over it. Cut a notch, shift the workpiece. Repeat until you have formed all the fingers. Repeat with the adjoining board. If you have adjusted the distance between the stop and the cutter properly, the notches in one board will interlock with the fingers on the other.

Materials List

FINISHED DIMENSIONS

PARTS

A. Face   ¾″ x 4½″ x 14½″
B. Stop   ½″* x ½″ x 1¾″

Change this dimension to ¼″ to make ¼″-wide finger joints.

HARDWARE

³⁄₁₆″ x 2½″ Carriage bolts**, flat washers, and wing nuts (2)

**The diameter and length of these bolts may change depending on the make of the miter gauge.*

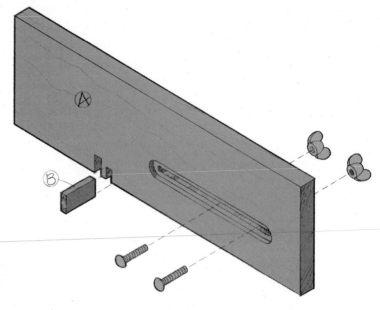

EXPLODED VIEW

1 Cut the parts.

Decide what size fingers you want to produce. The drawing shows a jig that cuts either ¼″- or ½″-wide fingers. However, you can cut almost any size, depending on the tool you use. A table-mounted router, using commonly available bits, will cut fingers ⅜″ and ¾″ wide, in addition to the sizes shown. It will also cut the tails for dovetail joints. (You'll have to cut the pins by hand.) Using a table saw and an ordinary combination blade, you can make ⅛″-wide fingers. Thin-kerf blades will make them as small as ¹⁄₁₆″. With a *stacking* dado cutter accessory (blades and chippers), you can cut fingers in ¹⁄₁₆″ increments, from ⅛″ to ¹³⁄₁₆″. A *wobble* dado cutter (off-center blade) will make fingers *any* size between ⅛″ and ¹³⁄₁₆″.

With all the possibilities, you may want to make jigs for several different finger sizes. When you have settled on a size, cut the parts.

2 Cut the mounting slot.

Determine the length and location of the slot in the face, which is dictated by the positions of the mounting holes in your miter gauge. Attached to the miter gauge, the jig should rest on the work surface and extend 3″-5″ past the blade. The slot thus should be at the same height as the mounting holes, and allow the jig to move at least 1″ to the right *and* left.

Measure the gauge, from the bottom edge to the center of the mounting holes. This determines the distance of the slot from the bottom edge of the jig (Variable A on the *Front View*). Measure the distance between the holes and add 2″ — this is the length of the slot (Variable B). Place the miter gauge in the table slot and measure the distance from the edge of the gauge that's farthest from the blade to the mounting hole closest to that edge. Add 1″ — this is the distance from the farthest edge of the jig to the beginning of the slot (Variable C).

*1/Use an overhead routing jig to cut both the ¾″- and ¼″-wide portions of the stopped slot. A straightedge guides the workpiece under the jig. When you change bits, **don't change the position of the jig or the straightedge.** If the setup remains the same for both cuts, the ¼″ portion of the slot will be centered in the ¾″ portion.*

Lay out the slot on the jig. To form each end of the slot, drill a ¾″-diameter, ¼″-deep counterbore, then a ¼″-diameter hole through the counterbore. Cut a *stepped* slot with a router and the overhead routing jig shown in the Routing chapter. Using a ¾″ straight bit,

rout a ¾″-wide, ¼″-deep slot connecting the counterbores. Switch to a ¼″ straight bit and, without changing the setup, rout a ¼″-wide slot connecting the holes. (See Figure 1.) The wider slot will form a ¼″ step on either side of the narrower slot.

3 **Attach the stop.** Mount a bit or cutter in your table-mounted router or table saw. The width of the cut must be the same as the thickness of the finger you want to make. Adjust the height of the bit or cutter to ½″ above the table.

Attach the jig to your miter gauge with carriage bolts,

flat washers, and wing nuts. Place the gauge in the table slot and shift the jig as far as it will go *away* from the blade or cutter. Tighten the wing nuts.

Turn on the router or table saw, and cut a notch in the jig. Glue the stop in this notch, as shown in the *Exploded View.*

4 **Cut the notch for the bit or cutter.** Raise the height of the bit or cutter to ¾″. Loosen the wing nuts and shift the jig toward the bit/cutter. Using a scrap piece of the stop as a spacer, adjust the jig align-

ment so the next cut will be one thickness of the stop away from the first cut. Tighten the wing nuts and make the second notch.

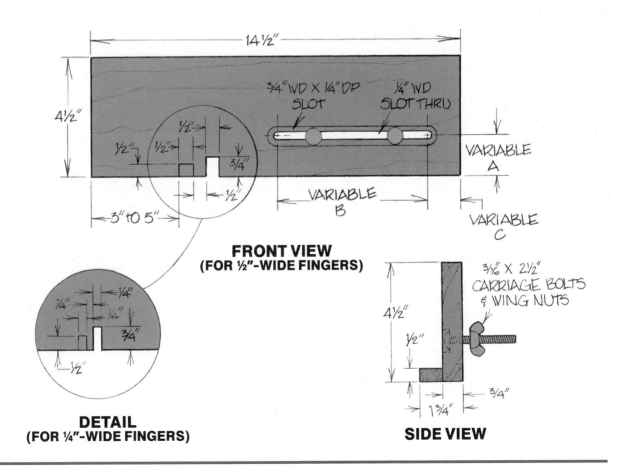

FRONT VIEW
(FOR ½″-WIDE FINGERS)

DETAIL
(FOR ¼″-WIDE FINGERS)

SIDE VIEW

Tips for Using the Finger Jig

The procedure for using the jig is straightforward. As described earlier, you simply use the stop to space the fingers as you cut them. There are, however, a few tricks you should know:

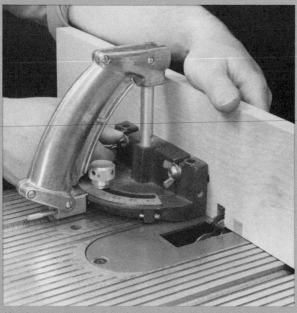

*Use the second notch to set the **approximate** position of the jig on the miter gauge each time you attach it. Put the notch over the bit/cutter and tighten the wing nuts. Make fine adjustments by cutting test pieces and shifting the jig right or left as needed.*

*To prevent the bit or cutter from tearing the wood on the back side of each cut, score the wood across the grain. This score must be **exactly** the same distance from the end of the board as the length of the fingers you will cut.*

*To further reduce tear-out, back up the workpiece with a scrap while you cut. The end of the scrap must be **without** fingers. You'll need a fresh, uncut scrap for every board you want to cut.*

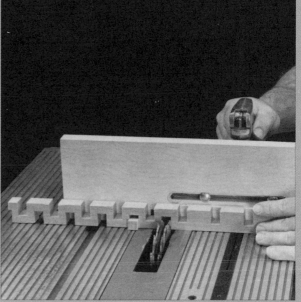

In addition to finger joints, you can also use this jig to make evenly spaced dadoes, grooves or notches in a workpiece. These, in turn, can be made to interlock with other workpieces. You can also use them by themselves or rip them into thinner pieces to form decorative moldings.

Tenoning Jig

To make cuts in the ends of boards, you must hold the board *vertically,* with the end resting on the saw or router table. The board can be difficult to control — particularly long, narrow workpieces such as frame parts and table legs. Neither the rip fence nor the miter gauge provides adequate support.

To make these cuts safely and accurately, use a tenoning jig. This is a tall extension that *rides along the fence.* Adjust the jig's dimensions so it fits snugly over the rip fence. (If you use this fixture on a router table, you will have to make a special fence.) Fit the jig over the fence, and position the pivot to hold the wood at the proper angle to the blade or cutter. Secure the workpiece in the jig with the quick-release clamp. Then turn the power on, and push the jig forward.

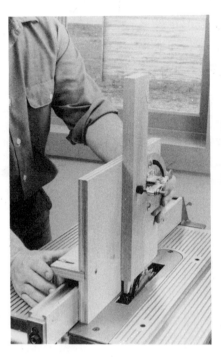

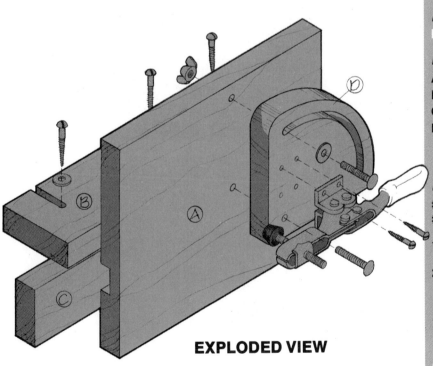

EXPLODED VIEW

Materials List

FINISHED DIMENSIONS

PARTS

A.	Extension	¾" x 8" x 9"
B.	Brace	¾" x 3⅛" x 9"
C.	Guide	¾" x (variable) x 9"
D.	Pivot	¾" x 4¾" x 4¾"

HARDWARE

#10 x 1¼" Flathead wood screws (3)

#12 x 1½" Roundhead wood screws and washers (3)

¼" x 2" Carriage bolts, flat washers, and wing nuts (2)

2¼" Quick-release clamp* and mounting screws

These can be purchased from most mail-order woodworking suppliers. They are sometimes called horizontal toggle clamps.

1

Cut the parts.   Measure the height and width of your table saw rip fence to make sure this jig will fit. As shown, the jig will accommodate a fence from ¾″ to 2″ wide, and up to 8″ high. The fences of most table saws fall within these dimensions, but it's good to check — yours could be the oddball.

Add ¼″ to the height of the fence — this will give you the width of the guide. It will also locate the groove in the extension. After you check your dimensions, cut the parts.

Use cabinet-grade plywood for the extension, brace, and guide, and a clear hardwood stock for the pivot.

2

Make the brace.   Lay out the open slots on the brace, as shown in the *Top View.* Drill a ³/₁₆″

hole to make the blind end of each slot. Cut the slots with a band saw or saber saw.

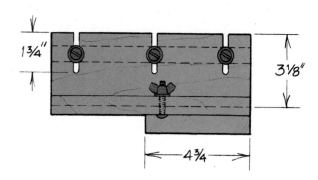

TOP VIEW

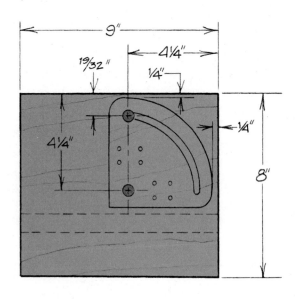

FRONT VIEW

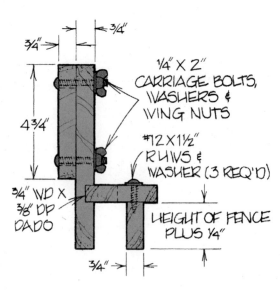

SIDE VIEW

3 **Make the pivot.**   Lay out the pivot on the stock as shown in the *Pivot Layout*. Drill a ¼″-diameter hole for the pivot bolt, and a ⁵⁄₁₆″-diameter hole to make each end of the curved slot. Also drill ⅛″ pilot holes *through* the stock, so you can mount the clamp on either side of the pivot and beside either straight edge. **Note:** The pivot is reversible; you can mount it in four different positions — facing forward or back, with the square corner up or down. When you change the position of the pivot, you may want to move the clamp, too.

   Cut the slot with a saber saw, and file the inside edges smooth. Last, cut the shape with a band saw or a saber saw, and sand the outside edges smooth.

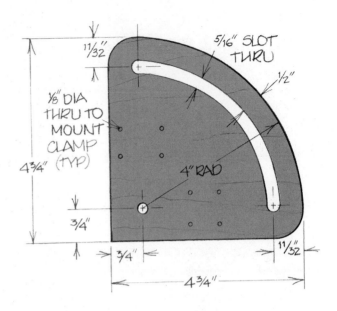

PIVOT LAYOUT

4 **Cut and drill the extension.**   Cut a ¾″-wide, ⅜″-deep groove in the back of the extension. Drill ¼″-diameter mounting holes for the pivot, as shown in the *Side View*.

5 **Assemble the parts.**   Glue the brace in the groove with the open slots facing away from the extension. Let the glue dry, then clamp the guide to the brace. The guide's outside face and the brace's outside edge should be flush. Drill pilot holes in the guide, directly under each open slot. Insert a roundhead screw with a washer in each slot, and drive it into the guide. Turn the screw so it's snug, but not tight.

   Attach the pivot to the extension with carriage bolts, washers, and wing nuts. Pass one bolt through the pivot hole, and another through the slot. Check the action of the pivot. If it binds on the slot bolt, file away a little wood from inside the slot.

   Tighten the wing nuts. Screw the quick-release clamp to the pivot so it overhangs one straight edge.

6 **Adjust the guide to fit the fence.**   Place the jig on the table saw, over the rip fence. Hold the extension firmly against one side of the fence, and push the guide against the other. Let go of the jig and tighten the roundhead screws. Check that the jig slides smoothly along the fence with no play.

   Ensure that the jig is perpendicular to the saw table. Plane a little stock from the bottom edge of the guide or extension, if necessary, to square it up.

   Note: As mentioned, you'll have to make an auxiliary fence for the router table to guide the jig. The router table fence probably won't do — most of these are too wide or have too many protrusions. To save setup time, rip this auxiliary fence the same height and width as your table saw fence. Cut it as long as the router table, and clamp it in place.

Tips for Using the Tenoning Jig

The tenoning jig will aid in making a variety of end cuts — tenons, dovetails, and open mortises, to name a few. When making any of these, you will find a common problem: the cutter or the bit tears the grain at the back of the cut.

You can do either of two things to prevent this. One is to score across the grain where the cutter will emerge; the surface fibers won't tear as the cutter hits them because they are *already* cut. The second trick is to back up the workpiece with an uncut scrap.

Score the wood across the grain where the cutter will emerge. The score must be the same distance from the end of the stock as the cutter's height above the table. This will cut the wood grain cleanly before it can tear.

Back up each cut with a scrap. This will brace the wood grain where the blade exits the stock. To provide the proper reinforcement, this scrap must be uncut. To make the square tenon shown, you need two scraps with uncut ends — one end for each cut.

1

To precisely center a slot mortise in the end of a board, make it in two cuts. Adjust the fence and the cutter to make just half the slot. Put the board in the tenoning jig and make the first pass.

2

Without moving the fence or the cutter, turn the board around in the jig, edge for edge, and make a second pass.

Credits

Although the jigs, fixtures, and shop furniture were all
built by the author, he does not claim credit for develop-
ing them. Most of these are common workshop designs.
The ideas were collected over the years from many,
many different woodworkers. The author is grateful to
these people for sharing their knowledge. In particular,
he thanks R. J. DeCristoforo, Bill Hylton, Jim McCann,
John Sill, John Shoup, David T. Smith, and the author's
grandfather, Willard Sizemore.

Rodale Press, Inc., publishes AMERICAN WOODWORKER™, the magazine for the serious woodworking hobbyist. For information on how to order your subscription, write to AMERICAN WOODWORKER™, Emmaus, PA 18098.